More Prayers

that

Change Things

More Prayers

that

Change Things

Lloyd Hildebrand

BRIDGE
LOGOS

Newberry, FL 32669

Bridge-Logos

Newberry, FL 32669

More Prayers That Change Things

By Lloyd Hildebrand

Printed in the United States of America.

Cover/Interior design by Kent Jensen | knail.com

Library of Congress Catalog Card Number: 2016937554

International Standard Book Number: 978-1-61036-157-6

Unless otherwise noted, all Scripture quotations are from the
King James Version of the Holy Bible.

Scripture quotations marked NKJV are taken from the New
King James Version of the Bible. Copyright 1979, 1980, 1982,
by HarperCollins.

Dedication

To everyone who read and appreciated the original book in this series, Prayers That Change Things, *as well as the other six books in the series. Thank you for your kind reviews and comments. To know that the book has ministered to you in so many ways greatly blesses my heart. My prayer is that* More Prayers That Change Things *will help you to go deeper in your walk with God and that He will bring about the changes you are looking for.*

"Whatever things you ask in prayer, believing, you will receive"

(JESUS, MATTHEW 21:22 NKJV)

Contents

Introduction

More Prayers That Change Things is the sequel to my first book in this series, *Prayers That Change Things*, which was originally published in 2012. If you have not read the first book, I encourage you to do so.

The original book, like this one, has to do with praying the Scriptures regarding various challenges and circumstances that people desire to change in their lives. The focus of the first book and this one is upon how praying the Word helps to change our lives in so many positive ways. God has an answer for every challenge, and we will find His answers in His Word. When we pray the Scriptures we are actually praying God's promises into existence, we are receiving His answers while we pray, and positive changes do come about in our lives and circumstances.

Change is constant, but it is not necessarily ever easy. When we change our thoughts we change our world. Peter Senge wrote, "People don't resist change. They resist being changed." Many people fear change, but I believe change is to be embraced, not feared. I can assure you that praying God's Word will change you in important ways.

Powerful resources are available to enable us to face change with faith and to accept the changes that come our way. One of these vital resources is the Word of God: "For the word of God is quick and powerful, and sharper than any two-edged sword, piercing even to the dividing asunder of soul and spirit, and of the joints and marrow, and is a discerner of the thoughts and intents of the heart" (Hebrews 4:12).

A second resource that is always available to us is prayer. Prayer is very powerful in helping us when we are facing changes in our lives. It is also a way to bring about the positive transformations that we desire. The Bible says, "Let us therefore come boldly unto the throne of grace, that we may obtain mercy, and find grace to help in time of need" (Hebrews 4:16).

A time of need in our lives might well be when we are facing something associated with change. The changes God institutes in our lives have an all-encompassing goal in mind: "For whom he did foreknow, he also did predestinate to be conformed to the image of his Son, that he might be the firstborn among many brethren" (Romans 8:29).

The prayers in this book are built directly from the Bible. They are based on some of the things that many people would like to change about themselves and these prayers seek God's help in doing so. The prayers are arranged in alphabetical order.

Combining the power of God's Word with the power of prayer always brings about positive changes in the believer's life. I know this from experience. Therefore, the prayers of this book are focused on changing our lives in positive ways.

As you pray the prayers contained within this book, you will be changed. Your mind will be renewed by "the washing of water by the word" (Ephesians 5:26).

Your faith will grow. Your understanding of spiritual truths will increase. You will be blessed beyond your wildest expectations. Approach these prayers with a sense of expectation, knowing that:

- Every time we open the Bible God speaks to us if we are listening.
- Every time we pray the Scriptures our faith grows.
- Every time we study the Word of God we grow in grace and love.
- Every time we meditate upon the Scriptures we are encouraged.
- Every time we reach out to God He responds in wonderful ways.
- Every time we seek God we find Him.
- Every time we ask He answers.
- Every time we worship Him we are changed in marvelous ways.
- Every time we listen to His Word we grow closer to Him.
- Every time we choose to follow His ways we are blessed.

The above list gives but a few of the benefits you will receive as you use this book in your personal prayer life. This method of prayer will fill your heart with gratitude. A very effective prayer is: "Yes, Lord," because to say yes to God is to line up your perspective with His will, His Word, and His ways.

As you see God answering your prayers about change, you will experience the joy of the Lord, which is your strength. (See Nehemiah 8:10.) You will get to know the Lord in exciting ways. Your soul will be renewed and your whole life will change.

As you will see, I have personalized the Scriptures in this book to make them more meaningful for you. You are about to discover a whole new approach to God. These prayers will help you to walk in His ways and to become victorious as you face challenges and changes. These prayers will lead you to succeed.

As you pray the prayers within this book, God's Word will come alive in new ways to you. You will hear His voice speaking to you. There is a sense in which you will receive answers to your prayers as you pray. Why does this happen? It's really quite simple. When you pray God's Word you are praying His will, and this is the key to answered prayer. The Bible says, "And this is the confidence that we have in him, that, if we ask any thing according to his will, he heareth us: and if we know that he hears us, whatsoever we ask, we know that we have the petitions that we desired of him" (1 John 5:14-15).

We can know that God hears us when we pray His Word. We can know that He is granting our petitions while we pray. This gives us great confidence in the power of His Word and the power of prayer. Putting the Bible into our prayers provides us with a faith-building and dynamic approach to God and all of life.

As you pray these prayers, I encourage you to include your own personal petitions within them. God promises, "Delight thyself also in the Lord; and he shall give thee the desires of thine heart" (Psalm 37:4). What a wonderful promise this is. God will give you the desires of your heart when you delight yourself in Him.

By praying the Scriptures your focus and your perspective will change. First and foremost, your focus will be on God and this focus changes everything. Oswald Chambers wrote, "We have to pray with our eyes on God, not on the difficulties." Do you see how important this is?

God always answers believing prayer that is based upon the promises of His Word. His promises are numerous, and you will find many of them in the prayers of this book. My hope is that you will get closer to God as you pray the prayers within this book and that you will grow in the grace and knowledge of Jesus Christ. (See 2 Peter 3:18.)

Fenelon wrote, "Time spent in prayer is never wasted." He is exactly right, for prayer changes us on the inside. It improves our outlook, and it builds our relationship with God. It changes our thoughts and the way we deal with the circumstances of life.

"Now unto him that is able to do exceeding abundantly above all that we ask or think, according to the power that worketh in us, unto him be glory in the church by Christ Jesus throughout all ages, world without end. Amen" (Ephesians 3:20-21).

PART I

The Benefits of Praying God's Word

Blessed is the man that walketh not in the counsel of the ungodly, nor standeth in the way of sinners, nor sitteth in the seat of the scornful. But his delight is in the law of the Lord; and in his law doth he meditate day and night. And he shall be like a tree planted by the rivers of water, that bringeth forth his fruit in his season; his leaf also shall not wither; and whatsoever he doeth shall prosper.

(PSALM 1:1-3)

Multitudinous benefits are to be derived from praying God's Word. We see some of these benefits in the above verses: stability, fruitfulness, and prosperity in every area of life. As we pray the Scriptures, we are meditating upon God's truths, and this is a wonderful way to saturate our minds with the words and ways of God.

Doing so brings wonderful changes to our lives, and these changes are the benefits that we will review in this chapter. The title of my book is *More Prayers That Change Things*, but it could just as well be entitled, *More Prayers That Change Lives*. Let me assure you that your life will change in vital ways as you learn to pray God's Word.

YOUR MIND WILL BE RENEWED

Praying God's Word causes you to think about things differently; it changes your perspective. The Bible says, "Seek ye the Lord while he may be found, call ye upon him while he is near. . . .For my thoughts are not your thoughts, neither are your ways my ways, saith the Lord" (Isaiah 55:6-8).

How vast is the gap between the human approach to things and God's approach. The gulf between our thoughts and His is deep and wide, and praying the Scriptures is a sure way to bridge that gap.

When we begin to look at things through the eyes of faith, everything begins to change. We approach problems differently. We become more positive. We are less fearful. We turn away from sin.

"Thy word have I hid in mine heart, that I might not sin against thee" (Psalm 119:11). As we pray His Word, we turn away from sin, and we begin walking in His truth and wisdom.

Paul wrote, "I beseech you therefore, brethren, by the mercies of God, that ye present your bodies a living sacrifice, holy, acceptable unto God, which is your reasonable service. And be not conformed to this world: but be ye transformed by the renewing of your mind, that ye may prove what is that good, and acceptable, and perfect, will of God" (Romans 12:1-2).

Total transformation comes to our lives when we begin to focus on God's Word in our prayer life and our daily life. Our minds are truly renewed, and such mental renewal brings renewal to everything we engage in. We see things differently. We feel differently, and we deal with others differently. These are just some of the things that result from praying the Scriptures and meditating upon them as we pray.

By spending time in God's Word our minds are renewed to such an extent that "we have the mind of Christ" (1 Corinthians 2:16). His mind, as we have already pointed out, is so different from our own. Jesus' focus was always centered on love and devotion to His heavenly Father. He does not want any person to perish. He wants all to come to salvation through faith.

How does this miraculous transformation of our minds and lives take place? How does His mind become our mind? The Bible says, "That he might sanctify and cleanse it [the Church] with the washing of water by the word" (Ephesians 5:26). This is how our minds are renewed and how we receive the mind of Christ—by the washing of water by the Word.

Our minds are cleansed and washed as we pray God's Word. Bathing and soaking in the truths of

God's Word through prayer, meditation, and worship brings amazing changes into our lives. Yes, I highly recommend this form of prayer; it does bring changes to our lives and our circumstances.

YOUR FAITH WILL GROW

Faith enables us to believe, receive, and hold tight to all God's promises, and there are thousands of personal promises in His Word. The Bible says, "Faith cometh by hearing, and hearing by the word of God" (Romans 10:17). There is no doubt about it, the Word of God is the source of our faith and by praying and meditating upon it our faith grows and strengthens.

What is biblical faith? The Bible says, "Faith is the substance of things hoped for, the evidence of things not seen" (Hebrews 11:1). Faith gives substance to our hope. As our faith grows, spiritual evidence develops within us.

This results in us knowing that God exists even though we cannot see Him. It helps us to understand His spiritual precepts and principles. It gives us solid ground on which to walk by faith and not by sight. Praying God's Word enables us to "stand fast in the faith" and to "be strong." (See 1 Corinthians 16:13).

Faith gives us a new perspective on life. It helps us to rise above our challenges. It gives us an entire new way of looking at everything.

Through faith we are able to please God: "Without faith it is impossible to please him: for he that cometh to God must believe that he is, and that he is a rewarder of them that diligently seek him" (Hebrews 11:6).

I believe these words of Dr. Martin Luther King, Jr.: "Faith is taking the first step even when you don't see the whole staircase." Faith enables us to see the invisible and to believe the truths of the Bible. It motivates you to keep going in God's direction.

Men and women of faith throughout the Bible have been people of valor and victory, as we see in the following examples from Faith's Hall of Fame (Hebrews 11):

- Enoch was translated
- Noah built an ark and because he obeyed God; he and his family (and the animals) were safe during the Flood
- Abraham sojourned in the land of promise
- Sarah received strength to conceive when she was way past age
- Moses endured, as "seeing Him who is invisible" (Hebrews 11:27)
- The Israelites passed through the Red Sea

The Bible says, "These all died in faith, not having received the promises, but having seen them afar off" (Hebrews 11:13). That is the meaning of faith—continuing to believe without seeing. The world says, "Seeing is believing," but the believer says, "Believing is seeing." What we see by faith brings excitement and expectation into our lives.

Faith provided so much for ancient people, and it

can do the same for us today. Here are some of the things that faith can do, based on Hebrews 11:

- Subdue kingdoms
- Bring about righteousness
- Fulfill God's promises
- Provide strength
- Enliven hope
- Encourage hearts
- Give us eternal life

These are just some of the many things faith can do for us. The list truly seems endless. The Apostle John wrote, "For whatsoever is born of God overcometh the world; and this is the victory that overcometh the world, even our faith" (1 John 5:4).

C.S. Lewis wrote, "I believe in Christianity as I believe that the sun has risen: not only because I see it, but by it I see everything else." Faith brings so many positive changes to our lives.

PEACE WILL BE IMPARTED TO YOU

The Prophet Isaiah wrote, "Thou wilt keep him in perfect peace, whose mind is stayed on thee; because he trusteth in thee" (Isaiah 26:3). Perfect peace! Could we ask for anything more? The Bible says we can have perfect peace in this world of sin. How is this possible? How do we obtain it? It comes in part from praying and meditating on God's Word.

It is so peaceful to soak our souls in the truths of God's Word. As we do so, He speaks to us and we hear Him whispering, "Peace is yours." This kind of peace is far different from anything the world has to offer. (See John 14:27.) It is peace like a river—perfect peace, and it removes all anxiety from our lives.

George Macdonald wrote, "A perfect faith would lift us absolutely above fear." This is true peace, and it is the rest that God promises to us.

The Bible says, "Be anxious for nothing; but in everything by prayer and supplication with thanksgiving let your requests be made known to God" (Philippians 4:6). Notice what happens when you pray in this way: "And the peace of God, which passeth all understanding, shall keep your hearts and minds through Christ Jesus" (Philippians 4:7). Peace of mind, peace of heart, and full spiritual peace are yours when you pray God's Word.

This kind of blessed peace implies a sense of security that comes from knowing that God hears you and wants to bless you. "But thou, when thou prayest, enter into thy closet, and when thou hast shut thy door, pray to thy Father which is in secret; and thy Father which seeth in secret shall reward thee openly" (Matthew 6:6).

This is spiritual knowledge that comes to us through faith and results in peace. It is peace like a river. It cleanses our souls and reenergizes our spirits. God's peace is so wonderful.

IT REMOVES ALL FEAR

The Bible provides us with our biggest defense against fear. It assures us that we have been adopted by our heavenly Father. "For ye have not received the spirit of bondage again to fear; but ye have received the Spirit of adoption, whereby we cry, Abba, Father" (Romans 8:15).

The word "Abba" is rarely used in the Scriptures. It means that God is our loving Father. It connotes intimacy with One who is like a daddy to us. Isn't it wonderful to know that God loves us so much that He has adopted us into His family? Being in the family of God keeps us from the bondage and torment caused by fear.

The best antidote against fear is love, as the Apostle John points out. Perfect love casts out all fear. (See 1 John 4:18). Yes, there is no fear in love, and since God is love we never need to fear when we are walking with Him. He will always hold our hand and lead us through even the darkest night.

Charles H. Brent wrote, "Peace comes when there is no cloud between us and God." Praying the Scriptures removes the clouds, and we draw very close to our heavenly Father.

God's perfect love combined with faith forms a strong defense against fear in all its ugly forms. It actually forms an impenetrable wall against fear. By praying God's Word we are building a sure defense against fear. We are finding a freedom that keeps us from all fear.

Fear is a form of sin, and the Bible says, "Thy word have I hid in my heart, that I might not sin against thee" (Psalm 119:11). Through praying the Bible we are hiding God's Word in our hearts, and this truly does keep us from sin.

YOU WILL DISCOVER GOD'S WILL

Corrie ten Boom wrote, "There are no 'ifs' in God's world. And no places that are safer than any other places. The center of His will is our only safety—let us pray that we may always know it." God's Word reveals His will to us.

Praying God's Word leads you to a full understanding of His perfect will both for yourself and for all believers. To know His will is to know His ways. Such knowledge helps us to walk in His ways at all times.

The Bible declares unto us the entire counsel of God. There simply is no better counsel to be had. With God and His Word as your counselor, you simply cannot fail. The Bible says, "Blessed is the man that walketh not in the counsel of the ungodly, nor standeth in the way of sinners, nor sitteth in the seat of the scornful. But his delight is in the law of the Lord; and in his law doth he meditate day and night" (Psalm 1:1-2).

What happens when we do this? "And he shall be like a tree planted by the rivers of water, that bringeth forth his fruit in his season; his leaf also shall not wither; and whatsoever he doeth shall prosper" (Psalm 1:3). All of this comes into our lives when we pray the Scriptures regularly. We are firmly planted.

Our leaf will not wither. And we will prosper in every possible way.

Clearly stated, here is God's will for you: ". . . to be conformed to the image of his Son" (Romans 8:29). When this happens, and praying God's Word greatly helps in this process, we are able to follow in the footsteps of the Master. "Be ye therefore followers of God, as dear children; and walk in love, as Christ also has loved us" (Ephesians 5:1).

As we pray the Scriptures, God speaks to us and reveals His will for us. He tells us what we are to do. He reveals His plans for us: "This book of the law shall not depart out of thy mouth; but thou shalt meditate therein day and night, that thou mayest observe to do according to all that is written therein: for then thou shalt make thy way prosperous, and then thou shalt have good success" (Joshua 1:8).

YOUR PRAYERS WILL BE ANSWERED AS YOU PRAY

God knows what you have need of even before you express it in prayer, and He wants to meet those needs. (See Matthew 6:8 and Philippians 4:19.) Remember this promise: "Fear not, little flock; for it is your Father's good pleasure to give you the kingdom" (Luke 12:22). What kingdom is Jesus referring to here? It is God's kingdom, which does not consist of meat or drink, but of righteousness, peace, and joy in the Holy Spirit. (See Romans 14:17.)

This kingdom is the Kingdom of Heaven. Jesus said, "Behold, the kingdom of God is within you" (Luke 17:21). All the treasures and glories of Heaven are within you now. Jesus prayed, "Thy kingdom come. Thy will be done in earth, as it is in heaven" (Luke 6:10).

These Scriptures show us how God answers our prayers when we utilize His Word. As you pray, He listens. Before you pray, He knows what you need. He wants you to express your needs to Him, to believe His Word, and to receive His promises. As you do so, you will notice several things happening:

1. You will be changed.
2. Things around you and within you will begin to change in positive directions.
3. You will understand His will.
4. He will lead you and direct your steps.

"Trust in the Lord, and do good; so shalt thou dwell in the land, and verily thou shalt be fed. Delight thyself also in the Lord; and he shall give thee the desires of thine heart. Commit thy way unto the Lord; trust also in him; and he shall bring it to pass" (Psalm 37:3-5).

Dietrich Bonhoeffer wrote, "The right way to pray is to stretch out our hands and ask of One who we know has the heart of a Father." That's our God, and He loves to bless His children.

YOUR LIFE WILL BEGIN TO CHANGE

What would you like to have changed in your life and circumstances? Most people seek happiness and joy. This is true spiritual prosperity. John wrote, "Beloved, I wish above all things that thou mayest prosper and be in health, even as thy soul prospereth" (3 John 2). Soul prosperity involves all God's blessings, including justification, redemption, forgiveness, joy, and love. God wants you to experience these precious gifts from His treasure trove. They are yours. All you have to do is take them by faith and walk in them.

Newness of life will be yours as you learn to walk in the Word and wisdom of God. The Word of God outlines how we should walk:

- In newness of life. (See Romans 6:4.)
- According to the Spirit. (See Romans 8:4.)
- Honestly. (See Romans 13:13-14.)
- By Faith. (See 2 Corinthians 5:7.)
- In Good Works. (See Ephesians 2:10.)
- Worthy of Our Calling. (See Ephesians 4:1-3.)
- In Jesus Christ. (See Colossians 2:6-7.)
- Not as Other Gentiles Walk. (See Ephesians 4:17-20.)
- In Love. (See Ephesians 5:1-2.)
- As Children of Light. (See Ephesians 5:8-10.)
- Circumspectly. (See Ephesians 5:15-16.)
- In Wisdom. (See Colossians 4:5.)
- Worthy of God. (See 1 Thessalonians 2:12.)
- In Truth. (See 2 John 4.)
- According to His commandments. (See 2 John 6.)
- In the Fear of the Lord. (See Acts 9:31.)

To walk as these Scriptures teach is to walk in the confidence of all God's special promises to you. This effects many positive changes in your life and circumstances, because it lifts you above the teachings and traditions of this world. It helps you to see that many of the things you thought before were not accurate.

Let God change your life through His Word. Praying His Word on a daily basis will cause these changes to manifest in your life, and you will become a different person.

YOU WILL LEARN AND MEMORIZE THE SCRIPTURES

Become familiar with God's Word, so familiar that you are able to recall His truths. You will be amazed by how many times certain Scriptures will come to your mind as you go about your daily duties. Sometimes you will be able to encourage others by telling them what God has to say about their circumstances.

Memorizing God's Word is really important. The Psalmist wrote, "Thy word have I hid in mine heart, that I might not sin against thee" (Psalm 119:9). This is only one of the benefits that come from Bible memorization, but it is surely an important one. Billy Graham wrote, "Sin will keep you from the Bible, but the Bible will keep you from sin."

When Jesus was tempted in the wilderness He combatted Satan with the Word of God, and Satan fled from Him every time He did so. When He told Satan, "It is written..." the devil fled the scene. He will do the same whenever you use the Word of God as your defensive weapon. God's Word is "the sword of the Spirit" (See Ephesians 6:17). It is a powerful sword indeed.

This sword is sharper than any other. The Bible says, "For the word of God is quick and powerful, and sharper than any two-edged sword, piercing even to the dividing asunder of soul and spirit, and of the joints and marrow, and is a discerner of the thoughts and intents of the heart" (Hebrews 4:12).

To say that God's Word is "quick" is to say that it is "alive." Yes, it is alive and powerful, and it is able to do so much, especially within us. It discerns the thoughts and intents of our hearts while dividing between our soul and spirit.

The soul is the seat of our emotions, will, and intellect, whereas the spirit is the place where God resides within us. It is important to know this distinction, and the Word of God makes it very clear indeed. It pierces so deep within us that it helps us to determine what our motives are and whether we are acting in accord with our souls or our spirits.

Learning and memorizing God's Word helps in another important area as well. Speaking the truth of God's Word when we are witnessing to others is much more effective than just sharing our own thoughts. The Bible says, "But sanctify the Lord God in your hearts: and be ready to give an answer to every man that asketh you a reason of the hope that is in you with meekness and fear" (1 Peter 3:15).

The reasons for your hope are found within the Word of God, and everyone needs to know what those reasons are.

YOU WILL REAP GOD'S PROMISES

As we pray God's Word, we meditate and reflect upon His promises. Faith comes to us, and we are able to receive His promises as we are praying. As I mentioned before, there are literally thousands of promises in the Bible, and each one is for you. What are some of those promises that your heavenly Father has given?

- You are forgiven. (See Ephesians 4:32.)
- You are saved. (See John 6:47.)
- Divine health is yours. (See Psalm 107:20.)
- Longevity is yours. (See Psalm 91:16.)
- You will live forever. (See John 3:16.)
- God's love for you is everlasting. (See Jeremiah 33:3.)
- Jesus is preparing a place for you. (See John 14:3.)
- You will be successful. (See Joshua 1:8.)
- You are never alone. (See Hebrews 13:5.)
- God is your strength. (See Psalm 118:14.)
- He gives His angels charge over you. (See Psalm 91:11.)
- He will deliver you. (See Psalm 91:3.)
- The Lord is your light and your salvation. (See Psalm 27:1.)
- The Lord is your Shepherd. (See Psalm 23:1.)

- The secret of the Lord is with you. (See Psalm 25:14.)
- The Lord is your rock. (See Psalm 18:2.)
- The joy of the Lord is your strength. (See Nehemiah 8:10.)
- Nothing will ever be able to separate you from God's love. (See Romans 8:38-39.)
- Christ lives within you. (See Colossians 1:27.)
- Faith is the victory. (See 1 John 5:4.)
- You are God's child. (See John 1:12.)
- God's power is always available to you. (See 2 Corinthians 13:4.)

The above list of more than twenty promises that come to us through the Word of God is just a miniscule portion of the promises we receive as we pray and meditate upon God's Word. Someone has said that there are more than 7,000 promises in the Bible, and I certainly believe this.

As I was preparing this section, I skimmed through some Bible verses, and I soon realized that I was building a list that would almost never end. I would encourage you to read the Bible with God's promises in mind. I believe you will be astounded by how many promises there are. Remember God wants you to know these promises, believe them, and receive them.

Dwight L. Moody said, "Tarry at a promise and God will meet you there." The prayers within this book will enable you to take your stand upon the promises, believe His promises, receive His promises, trust His promises, and expect His promises to be fulfilled in your life.

Through His promises you will meet with your heavenly Father.

PROFOUND JOY WILL COME TO YOU

As you pray God's Word, your heart will fill with joy. This is the joy that comes to all who know God and believe His Word. Doesn't it give you great joy to know that God hears your prayers and wants to have an intimate relationship with you?

David wrote, "And my soul shall be joyful in the Lord: it shall rejoice in his salvation" (Psalm 34:9). In this verse we see David making a choice. He is choosing to be positive and to direct his soul to be joyful in the Lord, and we can do the same.

Spending time in God's Word produces joy in your heart, because it leads you into the very presence of God. "Thou wilt shew me the path of life: in thy presence is fullness of joy; at thy right hand there are pleasures forevermore" (Psalm 16:11.)

Fullness of joy and pleasures forevermore are yours when you remain within God's presence. Praying His Word helps you to get there and to stay there. I can assure you that there is no better place to be.

Dwight L. Moody wrote, "The Lord gives His people joy when they walk in obedience to Him." So, walk in His presence and this will lead you to walk in obedience to Him. The end result will be abundant joy.

Let God be your exceeding joy. (See Psalm 43:4.) This is a choice you can make, and it will bring about the changes you seek. Hearing God's Word and receiving it bring joy to your heart. (See Matthew 13:20.) Receiving answers to your prayers enriches your joy.

In Jesus we find joy, "Whom having not seen, ye love; in whom, though now ye see him not, yet believing, ye rejoice with joy unspeakable and full of glory" (1 Peter 1:8).

As you pray God's Word you will receive God's unspeakable joy that is always full of glory.

YOU WILL EXPERIENCE A DEEPER LOVE FOR GOD AND OTHERS

As God's Word fills your heart, you will experience a depth of love you've never known before. Paul prayed, "That He would grant you, according to the riches of his glory, to be strengthened with might by his Spirit in the inner man; that Christ may dwell in your hearts by faith; that ye, being rooted and grounded in love, may be able to comprehend with all saints what is the breadth, and length, and depth, and height; and to know the love of Christ, which passeth knowledge, that ye might be filled with all the fullness of God" (Ephesians 3:16-19).

Wow! In these three verses we find at least five promises that are tied to love:

- You will be strengthened with might deep within.
- Christ will dwell within your heart by faith.
- You will be rooted and grounded in love.
- You will comprehend the love of Christ with all the saints.
- You will be filled with all the fullness of God.

To really know and believe these truths should fill your heart with love and joy. Let this overarching truth sink into your heart and soul: God loves you! When you let this sink in, your life will truly change, and you will want others to know and experience His love as well.

John wrote, "We love him, because he first loved us" (1 John 4:19). God is love. To know Him is to love Him. To love Him is to love others (and ourselves). "In this was manifested the love of God toward us, because that God sent his only begotten Son into the world, that we might live through him" (1 John 4:9).

I greatly appreciate what Saint Augustine wrote, "God loves each of us as if there were only one of us." Take a moment to think of that. He loves us as if we were His only child. What a thought. What a truth.

The apostle John then went on to say, "If God so loved us, we ought also to love one another" (1 John 4:11). The heart of the gospel is love. When we take a close look at the Word of God, we soon discover that it's all about love. Love is the bond of perfection. (See Colossians 3:14.) Love is the supreme commandment. (See Matthew 22:37-39.) Love never fails. (See 1 Corinthians 13:8.)

"And now abideth faith, hope, charity, these three; but the greatest of these is charity [love]" (1 Corinthians 13:13). Love is the most excellent way of all. (See 1 Corinthians 12:31.)

Thank God for His great love for us. Where would we be without it?

YOUR CONFIDENCE IN GOD WILL GROW

Confidence involves a firm belief, trust, reliance, and assurance. It comes to us, at least in part, from experience. This is certainly true with regard to our confidence in God. The Word of God and our experience help us to know that God is faithful, that His promises can be counted on, and that He will not fail us. We can depend on Him.

Floyd McClung wrote, "The kind of devotion that God delights in comes about when a person finds security in the pure, unselfish love of God. We don't find our security or our value from the rules we obey or the way we live. But in the love of God, we know that there is nothing we can do to make Him love us more or less—He just loves us!" This knowledge gives us great confidence.

The Bible says, "This I recall to my mind, therefore have I hope. It is of the Lord's mercies that we are not consumed, because his compassions fail not. They are new every morning: great is thy faithfulness. The Lord is my portion, saith my soul; therefore will I hope in him" (Lamentations 3:21-24).

We have reason to hope in Him, for our faith has substance. (See Hebrews 11:1.) Through faith and experience we know that God is always there for us. He will not let us down. He is our Father, and we are His children. He sees us in secret and He will reward us openly. (See Matthew 6:4.)

Take note of this prayer promise from Jesus: "Ask, and it shall be given you; seek, and ye shall find; knock, and it shall be opened unto you: for everyone that asketh receiveth; and he that seeketh findeth; and to him that knocketh it shall be opened. Or what man is there of you, whom if his son ask bread, will he give him a stone? Or if he ask a fish, will he give him a serpent? If ye then, being evil, know how to give good gifts unto your children, how much more shall your Father which is in heaven give good things to them that ask him?" (Matthew 7:7-11).

God is our Father, and the Aramaic word that is sometimes used for Him is "Abba." This is a term of tender endearment used by a beloved child; it is similar to "daddy" or "papa." It appears three times in the Bible:

1. Mark 14:36: Jesus prayed, "Abba, Father, all things are possible unto thee; take away this cup from me: nevertheless not what I will, but what thou wilt."
2. Romans 8:15-17: "For ye have not received the spirit of bondage again to fear; but ye have received the Spirit of adoption, whereby we cry, Abba Father. The Spirit itself beareth witness with our spirit, that we are children of God: and

if children, then heirs; heirs of God, and joint-heirs with Christ; if so be that we suffer with him, that we may be also glorified together."

3. Galatians 4:5-6: "To redeem them that were under the law, that we might receive the adoption of sons. And because ye are sons, God hath sent forth the Spirit of his Son into your hearts, crying, Abba, Father."

Jesus prayed to His Abba-Father, and now we are able to do so as well because we have been adopted into His family. Because we are God's adopted children, we have received a wonderful inheritance from Him, and we are joint-heirs with Christ. The Bible says, "In whom [Christ] we have obtained an inheritance, being predestinated according to the purpose of him who worketh all things after the counsel of his own will: that we should be to the praise of his glory, who also first trusted in Christ, in whom ye also trusted, after that ye heard the word of truth, the gospel of your salvation: in whom also after that ye believed, ye were sealed with that holy Spirit of promise, which is the earnest of our inheritance" (Ephesians 1:11-14).

For all these reasons and many more, we should be careful to hold on to our confidence. "Cast not away therefore your confidence, which hath great recompense of reward" (Hebrews 10:35). Let your confidence in God grow as you pray His Word. "For we are made partakers of Christ, if we hold the beginning of our confidence steadfast unto the end" (Hebrews 3:14).

Faith leads to trust, trust leads to confidence, and confidence leads to certainty. Yes, you can be certain that God will honor His Word to you. It will not return unto Him void. (See Isaiah 55:11.)

YOU WILL EXPERIENCE GOD'S BLESSINGS

Moses pointed out that obedience is a prerequisite to receiving God's blessings. He wrote, "And it shall come to pass, if thou shalt hearken diligently unto the voice of the Lord thy God, to observe and to do all his commandments which I command thee this day, that the Lord thy God will set thee high above all the nations of the earth: and all these blessings shall come on thee, and overtake thee, if thou shalt hearken unto the voice of the Lord thy God" (Deuteronomy 28:1-2):

- You will be blessed in the city and in the field.
- The fruit of your body, of your ground, and of your livestock will be blessed.
- Your basket and your store shall be blessed.
- You will be blessed when you come in and when you go out.
- Your enemies will be smitten.
- The Lord will command His blessing in your storehouse and in all the work that you do.
- He will establish you in holiness.
- He will make you plenteous in goods.
- He will open His good treasure unto you.
- He will bless the work of your hands.

- You will be a lender, not a borrower.
- You will be the head, not the tail.
- You will be above and not beneath.

These affirmations from Deuteronomy 28:1-14 represent only a small portion of the blessings God has in store for you because He loves you.

Paul wrote, "Blessed be the God and Father of our Lord Jesus Christ, who hath blessed us with all spiritual blessings in heavenly places in Christ" (Ephesians 1:3).

Every spiritual blessing is yours already. You are the blessed child of God. All He asks of you is to trust Him and obey Him.

Therefore, pray His Word, for this method of praying will show you what He expects of you and enable you to trust Him for all that you need.

Why does He want to bless you in so many ways? He is your Father and He knows that as you become a blessing to others, you will be blessed. He wants you to know that He is always there for you. He loves you with an everlasting love. He wants you to pass His blessings on to your children and grandchildren. He wants to have intimate fellowship with you.

Our Father is a blessing-oriented God. He loves to give good things to His children. Francis Chan wrote, "True faith means holding nothing back. It means putting every hope in God's fidelity to His promises."

We have discussed thirteen of the benefits of praying God's Word in this chapter, but there are many more. As you pray the prayers in this book, you will personally experience the benefits God wants you to have and your life will change in so many wonderful ways.

Here is a list of some other benefits you will receive as you pray God's words:

- You will pray God's promises into existence
- You will gain spiritual insights and understanding
- You will be reminded of all God has done, is doing, and will do in your life
- You will be impelled to share His truths with others
- You will be comforted
- You will be spiritually restored
- You will have a more abundant life

Isn't it wonderful to know that these blessings are your inheritance as a child of God who knows His Word and prays His promises? There are additional blessings that will come your way as you learn to use this style of prayer. Be prepared for wonderful discoveries as you pray.

PART II

Personalized Prayers From the Bible

Pray without ceasing.

(1 THESSALONIANS 5:17)

Many years ago I learned to personalize God's Word as I used it in prayer, worship, study, preaching, teaching, and witnessing. This approach enables us to understand that God is speaking to us as individuals and as a body of believers through His Word, and this helps us to understand what the Father is saying to us.

The Bible contains many prayers and each one is there for several purposes. Some teach us how to pray while others show us the kinds of things we should pray for. Each one reveals certain keys to answered prayer.

This chapter deals with many prayers from the Bible. After quoting the prayers, I've personalized them so you can pray them for yourself. This is a wonderful way to pray, because as you pray, God will answer you.

There is a sense in which He actually has to answer you because you are praying His Word and His will for your life. Remember, His Word will never return to Him empty. God declares, "So shall my word be that goeth forth out of my mouth: it shall not return unto me void, but it shall accomplish that which I please, and it shall prosper in the thing whereto I sent it" (Isaiah 55:11).

There are several prayers printed in the Bible. In the following pages I've quoted some of them, discussed them, and personalized them so that they will have special, personal meaning for you.

1. THE LORD'S PRAYER

After this manner therefore pray ye: Our Father which art in heaven, hallowed be thy name. Thy kingdom come. Thy will be done in earth, as it is in heaven. Give us this day our daily bread. And forgive us our debts, as we forgive our debtors. And lead us not into temptation, but deliver us from evil: for thine is the kingdom, and the power, and the glory, forever. Amen.

(MATTHEW 6:9-13)

Our Lord Jesus prayed this prayer in order to show us how to pray, and it is a good model to follow whenever you pray. Note that it begins with adoration of our heavenly Father. His name is to be hallowed [held as holy] at all times.

Please note that Jesus uses plural pronouns in this prayer and in this way He is including each one of us. It is an intercessory prayer for us and for the entire Body of Christ.

He then asks for God's kingdom to come. There is a sense in which God's kingdom has already come, is coming, and will come. His kingdom is within you. (See Luke 17:21.) At the end of the age, God's kingdom will be established here on Earth, and that will be a glorious time of peace, love, and joy.

Jesus asks for God's will to be done on Earth as it is in Heaven. What a different world it will be when that happens. In Heaven there is no pain, sorrow, hardship, sickness, or fear. I pray that we could experience the same here on Earth, and I believe it will happen one day. In the meantime, I believe He has made it possible for us to experience His kingdom in the here and now.

The next sentence in the Lord's Prayer asks for God to supply our needs. He will certainly do so. Paul wrote, "But my God shall supply all your need according to his riches in glory by Christ Jesus" (Philippians 4:19). The reality is that He has already supplied our needs through Jesus. We need to believe that, for such belief will help to remove all fear from our lives.

Forgiveness is the next subject in this wonderful prayer. Note that we can expect forgiveness in the same way that we forgive others. God wants us to learn to walk in forgiveness, for He knows that as we learn to forgive others, all bitterness toward them will vanish. We will experience spiritual freedom and joy as we do so.

Jesus asks the Father to deliver us from evil and all temptation. God will never tempt us, but He wants us to learn how not to yield to temptation. Paul wrote, "There hath no temptation taken you but such as is common to man: but God is faithful, who will not suffer you to be tempted above that ye are able; but will with the temptation also make a way to escape, that ye may be able to bear it" (1 Corinthians 10:13).

Jesus concludes this model prayer with praise to His Father by acknowledging that all things belong to Him. The Lord's Prayer gives us a good example of the way to pray, and I've personalized it as follows. Please note that I've added related thoughts from various Scriptures in the personalized versions of each of these prayers.

The Personalized Lord's Prayer

Heavenly Father, your name is holy and glorious. I adore you and I praise your name. Thank you for your kingdom, which is not meat and drink, but righteousness, peace, and joy in you. (See Romans 14:17.) I thank you that your kingdom is within me, and I look forward to the time when your kingdom will come to Earth. I pray that your will would be done in my life and upon this planet as well. I look forward to the time when there will no longer be any sickness, sorrow, pain, or fear. Thank you for this promise from your Word, Lord God.

You are always faithful to me. I thank you that you are my Shepherd. Therefore, I shall not want. Thank you for supplying all my needs according to your riches in glory by Christ Jesus. You have given me the innermost desires of my heart, and I thank you for all that you have given to me.

Help me to forgive others. I realize, Lord, that I can expect to be forgiven by you in the same way that I forgive others. I want to love others without any hypocrisy whatsoever, and I want to forgive those who have caused problems for me. Help me, also, Lord, to forgive myself for my failing. I thank you for the blood of Jesus Christ which cleanses me from all sin—past, present, and future.

I know you will not lead me into temptation, but when temptation tries to seduce me, I ask that you would deliver me, Father. Deliver me and my family from all evil as we find our hiding place in you.

There is such security in the knowledge that yours is the everlasting kingdom, the power, and the glory forever. Therefore, I have nothing to fear. In Jesus' name I pray, Amen.

2. THE SINNER'S PRAYER

God be merciful to me a sinner.

(LUKE 18:13).

This brief prayer was uttered by a tax collector who heard Jesus share one of His profound parables. This brought him under conviction. He realized that he was not righteous and he smote his breast and said, "God, be merciful to me a sinner."

In His parable Jesus had asked, "When the Son of man cometh, will he find faith on the earth?" He knew He was speaking to men (a Pharisee and a tax collector) who trusted that they were righteous in themselves. These men actually despised others.

After the tax collector uttered the Sinner's Prayer, however, he was cleansed of his sin and his self-righteousness. Jesus said, "I tell you, this man went down to his house justified rather than the other [the Pharisee]: for everyone that exalteth himself shall be abased; and he that humbleth himself shall be exalted" (Luke 18:14).

The Personalized Sinner's Prayer

Heavenly Father, forgive me of my sin, my pride, and my self-righteousness. I repent of these failings, and I surrender my life to you. Be merciful to me, for I know I am a sinner. As I confess my sins to you, I know you are forgiving me and cleansing me from all unrighteousness. (See 1 John 1:9.)

Thank you for sending Jesus to be the propitiation for my sins. He is my Savior, and I trust Him for all I need. Thank you for loving me so much that you sent Him to give me eternal and abundant life. (See John 3:16 and John 10.) Help me to humble myself in your presence, to realize how much I need you at all times, and to walk with you each step of my way.

I trust in you with all my heart and I will not lean upon my own understanding. In all my ways I will acknowledge you, and I know you will always direct me. (See Proverbs 3:5-6.) Jesus is the Lord of lords and the King of kings, and I thank you for raising Him from the dead. He is the resurrection and the life. It is so wonderful to know Him and to experience His resurrection power each day.

Thank you for saving me, Father. In Jesus' name I pray, Amen.

3. THE PRAYER OF JABEZ

Oh, that you would bless me indeed, and enlarge my territory, and that Your hand would be with me, and that You would keep me from evil, that I may not cause pain! So, God granted him what he requested.

(1 CHRONICLES 4:10 NKSJV)

We don't know a great deal about Jabez, but we do know he prayed with faith. He asked for God's blessing to be upon His life by enlarging his territory, keeping His hand with him, and keeping him from evil. This is a powerful prayer to personalize, believe, and receive. It is filled with good things that God wants to give to us.

Note that after Jabez prayed, the Lord gave him all that he requested. Jesus said, "Ask, and you will receive, seek and you will find, knock and the door will be opened." (See Matthew 7:7.) This is exactly what Jabez did, and God heard him and gave him the desires of his heart. He promises to do the same for you.

The Personalized Prayer of Jabez

Father, I thank you for being there for me. I know you hear me when I pray, and I know that you will grant my requests. Knowing these things, I ask that you would bless me indeed and that you would bless my family as well.

I believe all the promises of your Word, such as this one: "The blessing of the Lord maketh rich and He adds no sorrow with it" (Proverbs 10:22). Thank you, Father. To be blessed is to be happy, and your abundance in my life makes me happy indeed.

I take hold of your mighty hand, Father, and I know you will lead me and guide me each step of my way. You will not permit me to stumble or fall as I walk hand in hand with you.

Keep me from evil, Father, and help me to walk in the light as you are in the light. (See 1 John 1:7.) You are my light and my salvation. (See Psalm 27:1.) You are my high tower. (See Psalm 18:2.) You are my rock of refuge. (See Psalm 94:22.) Thank you for taking care of me at all times. In Jesus' name I pray, Amen.

4. A PRAYER OF ELIJAH

Hear me, O Lord, hear me, that this people may know that thou art the Lord God, and that thou hast turned their heart back again.

(1 KINGS 18:37).

In this prayer of the Prophet Elijah we discover his concern for the people, which was reflected brightly in this brief prayer. He besought the Lord to hear him. From his sincere, heartfelt prayer it is easy to discern that Elijah cared about people and that he believed deeply in God and His ability to turn things around.

This is a prayer of intercession in that Elijah was beseeching God to change the hearts of the people. The Lord heard his prayer, and notice what happened next: "Then the fire of the Lord fell, and consumed the burnt sacrifice, and the wood, and the stones, and the dust, and licked up the water that was in the trench. And when all the people saw it, they fell on their faces: and they said, The Lord, he is the God; the Lord, he is the God" (1 Kings 18:38-39).

Elijah prayed, the fire fell, and the people repented and acknowledged God. After hearing the prophet's prayer and seeing the mighty miracle that followed, the people turned their hearts back to God again. We need to be praying this same prayer today for the people of our nation and the world.

The Personalized Prayer of Elijah

Almighty God, I pray in Jesus' name that you would send revival to the Earth. I pray that people everywhere would know that you are the Lord their God and that they would turn their hearts back to you again.

I believe that when this happens, Father, everything in our world will change for the better. I ask that you would do what is necessary to fulfill this prayer. Hear me, O Lord, hear me, and heal our land and all the nations of the world.

Send your fires of revival and consume all the idols that people are serving.

I know you do hear me and that you are at work to bring this prayer to pass. Thank you so much. In Jesus' name I pray, Amen.

5. SOLOMON'S PRAYER AT THE DEDICATION OF THE TEMPLE

Lord God of Israel, there is no God like thee, in heaven above, or on earth beneath, who keepest covenant and mercy with thy servants that walk before thee with all their heart. . . . And now, O God of Israel, let thy word, I pray thee, be verified. . . . Yet have thou respect unto the prayer of thy servant, and to his supplication, O Lord my God, to hearken unto the cry and to the prayer, which thy servant prayeth before thee today: That thine eyes may be open toward this house night and day, even toward the place of which thou hast said, My name shall be there; that thou mayest hearken unto the prayer which thy servant shall make toward this place. And hearken thou to the supplication of thy servant, and of thy people Israel, when they shall pray toward this place: and hear thou in heaven thy dwelling place: and when thou hearest, forgive.

(1 KINGS 8:22-30).

Imagine what Solomon and the people of Israel were feeling on this great day. They were dedicating the Temple to the Lord. Solomon knew that God is a covenant-keeping God and that He wants His servants to walk before Him in integrity and trust.

He asked God to verify His Word, which He is still doing to this very day through His creation and many signs and wonders. He asked God to respect his prayer and to hearken unto his cry. He besought the Lord to let His name be in the Temple and that His eyes would ever be open toward the Temple.

He then asked for God to forgive him and the people of Israel. He went on to pray, "Give to every man according to his ways, whose heart thou knowest; (for thou, even thou only, knowest the hearts of all the children of men;) that they may fear thee all the days that they live in the land which thou gavest unto our fathers. . . .Hear thou in heaven thy dwelling place, and do according to all that the stranger calleth to thee for: that all the people of the earth may know thy name, to fear thee, as do thy people Israel; and that they may know that this house, which I have builded, is called by thy name" (1 Kings 8:39-43).

Solomon proceeds to ask God to help them when they go forth to battle, to maintain their cause, to forgive them, to lead them to repentance, and to bless them. He then blessed the people with this benediction: "Blessed be the Lord, that hath given rest unto his people Israel, according to all that he promised: there hath not failed one word of all his good promise" (1 Kings 8:56).

Solomon prayed for the world. He wanted everyone to know the God of Israel. Great faith must have risen in the hearts of the people who heard his prayer when he said, "There hath not failed one word of all His good promise" (1 Kings 8:56). It is important to realize that God still keeps His promises.

The Personalized Prayer of Solomon at the Dedication of the Temple

God, my Father, I thank you for keeping covenant and mercy with me. Help me to walk before you with all my heart. Let your Word be verified in my life, Lord, and let me walk in your Word each day. Please listen to my prayers and supplications. I know you hear me, and I thank you so much for always blessing me.

I pray that you will draw people everywhere to you, that you will lead people of all nations into a saving knowledge of Jesus Christ. Forgive us, Father, for failing to acknowledge you at all times. I am so glad to know that you know my heart and how I want to follow you. Help me to reverence you all the days of my life.

I honor your sacred name and your Word. Thank you for the rest you have given to me. I praise you that not one word of all your good promises has ever failed.

In Jesus' name I pray, Amen.

6. PAUL'S PRAYER FOR THE EPHESIANS

For this cause I bow my knees unto the Father of our Lord Jesus Christ, of whom the whole family in heaven and earth is named, that he would grant you, according to the riches of his glory, to be strengthened with might by his Spirit in the inner man; that Christ may dwell in your hearts by faith; that ye, being rooted and grounded in love, may be able to comprehend with all saints what is the breadth, and length, and depth, and height; and to know the love of Christ, which passeth knowledge, that ye might be filled with all the fullness of God. Now unto him that is able to do exceeding abundantly above all that we ask or think, according to the power that worketh in us, unto him be glory in the church by Christ Jesus throughout all ages, world without end"

(EPHESIANS 3:14-31).

What a powerful prayer this is. It is one of my favorite prayers in the entire Bible. The Great Apostle is praying for the people of Ephesus whom he loves deeply because they are his children in the faith. Imagine them receiving this letter and passing it from one to another. How blessed they must have felt when they heard this letter being read in their congregation.

I know God heard this prayer and responded by blessing the Ephesians with greater faith, love, strength, and hope, and this is what we need today.

The Personalized Prayer of Paul for the Ephesians

Lord God, I bow my knees before you, and I ask you to grant that I would be strengthened with all might by the Spirit deep within me, according to the riches of your glory. Thank you for letting Christ dwell in my heart by faith. I love Him so. You have rooted and grounded me in love so that I may comprehend with all saints the breadth, length, depth, and height of your love, which surely does surpass knowledge.

Fill me with all your fullness, Father. How I praise you for the fact that you are able to do exceeding abundantly above all that I could ever ask or think, according to the power that is at work within me. Unto you be glory in the Church by Christ Jesus throughout all ages, world without end. In Jesus' name I pray, Amen.

7. PAUL'S PRAYER FOR THE COLOSSIANS

For this cause we also, since the day we heard it, do not cease to pray for you, and to desire that ye might be filled with the knowledge of his will in all wisdom and spiritual understanding; that ye might walk worthy of the Lord unto all pleasing, being fruitful in every good work, and increasing in the knowledge of God; strengthened with all might, according to his glorious power, unto all patience and longsuffering with

joyfulness; giving thanks unto the Father,
which hath made us meet to be partakers of
the inheritance of the saints in light.

(COLOSSIANS 1:9-12)

Though this is an intercessory prayer for the Colossians, it is readily adaptable to becoming a personalized prayer for us to pray as individuals. This is a powerful prayer in which Paul asks God to fill the Colossians with the knowledge of His will. As we learn to pray His will as it is revealed in His Word, we will find answers to our prayers. God hears us when we pray according to His will. (See 1 John 5:14-15.)

After this prayer, Paul goes on to celebrate God's mighty attributes. He assures the Colossians of God's power to deliver them from the powers of darkness. He has translated us into the Kingdom of His dear Son in whom we have redemption through His blood and the forgiveness of our sins. This is a good time to read the entire first chapter of Colossians, for it is filled with God's promises to you.

The Personalized Prayer of Paul for the Colossians

Heavenly Father, thank you for your Word which contains so many wonderful promises for me to claim and examples for me to follow. I ask that you would fill me with the knowledge of your will in all wisdom and spiritual understanding.

I desire to walk worthy of you, Lord, unto all pleasing, being fruitful in every good work and increasing in my personal knowledge of you. Strengthen me with all might, Father, according to your glorious power, unto all patience and longsuffering with joyfulness. I give thanks to you for everything you have done, are doing, and will do in my life. Thank you for making me a partaker of the inheritance of the saints in light.

In Jesus' name I pray, Amen.

8. JUDE'S BENEDICTORY PRAYER

Now unto him that is able to keep you from falling, and to present you faultless before the presence of his glory with exceeding joy, to the only wise God our Saviour, be glory and majesty, dominion and power, both now and ever. Amen.

The Epistle of Jude contains only one chapter, and it is very brief. Nonetheless, it is packed with spiritual wisdom and vital insights. He admonishes the saints to earnestly contend for the faith, to build themselves up in the faith, to pray in the Holy Ghost, to keep themselves in the love of God, and to look for the mercy of the Lord Jesus Christ unto eternal life.

The chapter also contains promises for the believer to receive and appropriate in their own lives. He concludes the book with this benedictory prayer of blessing and praise.

The Personalized Benedictory Prayer of Jude

Heavenly Father, thank you for keeping me from falling.

I know that you will one day present me faultless before your presence with great joy. This is because you have justified me and made me righteous.

You are the only wise God, my Savior, and it is wonderful to meditate upon all your promises to me and to meditate upon who you are. Unto you be glory, majesty, dominion, and power both now and forever. In Jesus' name I pray, Amen.

9. DAVID'S PRAYER OF CONFESSION

Have mercy upon me, O God, according to thy lovingkindness: according unto the multitude of your tender mercies blot out my transgressions. Wash me thoroughly from mine iniquity, and cleanse me from my sin. For I acknowledge my transgressions; and my sin is ever before me. Against thee, thee only, have I sinned, and done this evil in thy sight; that thou mightest be justified when thou speakest, and be clear when thou judgest. Behold, I was shapen in iniquity; and in sin did my mother conceive me. Behold, thou desirest truth in the inward parts: and in the hidden part thou shalt make me to know wisdom. Purge me with hyssop, and I shall be clean: wash me, and I shall be whiter than snow. Make me to hear joy and gladness; that the bones which thou hast broken may rejoice. Hide thy face from my sins, and blot out all my iniquities. Create in me a clean heart, O God; and renew a right spirit within me. Cast me not away from your presence; and take not thy Holy Spirit from me. Restore unto me the joy of thy salvation; and uphold me with thy free spirit. Then will I teach transgressors thy ways; and sinners shall be converted unto thee. Deliver me from blood guiltiness, O God, thou God of my salvation: and my tongue shall sing aloud of thy righteousness. O Lord, open thou my lips; and my mouth shall show forth thy praise. For thou desirest not sacrifice; else would I give it: thou delightest not in burnt offering. The sacrifices of God are a broken spirit: a broken and a contrite heart, O God, thou wilt not despise. Do good in thy good pleasure unto Zion: build thou the walls of Jerusalem. Then shalt thou be pleased with the sacrifices of righteousness, with burnt offering and whole burnt offering; then shall they offer bullocks upon thine altar.

(PSALM 51:1-19)

Many of the Psalms are personal prayers to God, but this is perhaps the most personal one of all. David prayed this prayer after the prophet Nathan confronted him about his sexual affair with Bathsheba. It is clear that David is in deep remorse over his sin. Sin always separates us from God, and this separation is very painful to one who has known Him personally.

David asks for God's mercy and forgiveness, which are readily available to him (and to us). God loves us, understands us, and wants us to prosper in every way. That's why He sent Jesus to become the propitiation for our sins. When we learn how to wash ourselves in the blood of Jesus, we become whiter than snow.

David wanted to have fellowship with God and to know joy and gladness again, so he confessed his sin to the Lord. He prayed sincerely, "Create in me a clean heart, O God; and renew a right spirit within me" (Psalm 51:10). This is a good prayer to pray every day.

David knew he needed God's forgiveness and restoration if he was going to teach God's ways to other transgressors. He was a soul-winner, and he wanted people to come to a personal knowledge of God. Though his spirit was broken, he knew God was at work in his life.

(Please read my earlier book entitled, *Praying the Psalms Changes Things*, which was published by Bridge-Logos, Inc. in 2014.)

The Personalized Prayer of David's Confession

Heavenly Father, thank you for your mercy and grace. Have mercy upon me according to your lovingkindness. Wash me thoroughly from my iniquity and cleanse me from my sin. I acknowledge my transgressions, and my sin is ever before me.

Against you, and you only, have I sinned and done this evil in your sight. (Please acknowledge your personal transgressions here.)

I know you desire truth in my inward parts. Help me to know your wisdom deep within my soul. Purge me and I shall be clean. Wash me and I shall be whiter than snow. Help me to hear joy and gladness again. Create in me a clean heart, O God, and renew a right spirit within me. Do not cast me away from your presence, and do not take your Holy Spirit away from me.

Restore unto me the joy of your salvation, Lord, and uphold me with your free Spirit. Then will I teach your ways to transgressors, and sinners will be converted unto you.

Deliver me from my guilt, O God of my salvation, and my tongue will sing aloud about your righteousness and your love. Open my lips and my mouth will show forth your praise. I am so thankful, Father, that you will never despise a broken and a contrite heart.

In Jesus' name I pray, Amen.

10. DAVID'S PRAYER OF PRAISE AND REFLECTION

O Lord, thou hast searched me, and known me. Thou knowest my downsitting and mine uprising, thou understandest my thought afar off. Thou compassest my path and my lying down, and art acquainted with all my ways. For there is not a word in my tongue, but, lo, O Lord, thou knowest it altogether. Thou hast beset me behind and before, and laid thine hand upon me. Such knowledge is too wonderful for me; it is high, I cannot attain unto it. Whither shall I go from thy spirit? Or whither shall I flee from thy presence? If I ascend up into heaven, thou art there: if I make my bed in hell, behold, thou art there. If I take the wings of the morning, and dwell in the uttermost parts of the sea; even there shall thy hand lead me, and thy right hand shall hold me. If I say, surely the darkness shall cover me; even the night shall be light about me. Yea, the darkness hideth not from thee; but the night shineth as the day: the darkness and the light are both alike to thee. For thou hast possessed my reins: thou hast covered me in my mother's womb. I will praise thee; for I am fearfully and wonderfully made: marvelous are thy works; and that my soul knoweth right well. My substance was not hid from thee, when I was made in secret, and curiously wrought in the lowest parts of the earth. Thine eyes did see my substance, yet being unperfect; and in thy book all my members were written, which in continuance were fashioned, when as yet there was none of them. How precious also are thy thoughts unto me, O God! How great is the sum of them! If I should count them, they are more in number than the sand: when I awake, I am still with thee. Surely thou wilt slay the wicked, O God: depart from me therefore, ye bloody men. For they speak against thee wickedly, and thine enemies take thy name in vain. Do not I hate them, O Lord, that hate thee? And am I not grieved with those that rise up against thee? I hate them with perfect hatred: I count them mine enemies. Search me, O God, and know my heart: try me, and know my thoughts: And see if there be any wicked way in me, and lead me in the way everlasting.

(PSALM 139:1-24)

Clearly, David is very serious about his relationship with God. He wants everything in his relationship with the Lord to be above board, and he knows that God knows everything about him already, including his thoughts and feelings. God even knows the words that David will speak before he speaks them.

He points out that there is no place where one can hide from God, not even in Heaven or in hell. He is confident that God will guide him no matter where he is.

David reflects on the miracle of his birth, and He praises God for creating him. He concludes his prayer with a plea for God to search his heart and thoughts. He asks God to expose any wicked ways He may find within him, and he asks the Father to lead him in the everlasting way.

The Personalized Prayer of David as He Praises and Meditates Upon God

Heavenly Father, thank you for searching me and knowing me. You know everything about me, and you understand all my thoughts. You know what words I will speak. Such knowledge is quite overwhelming to me, and I know I cannot attain to it.

Thank you for always being with me. I never want to leave your presence, Father. Thank you for covering me in my mother's womb. I will praise you, for I know I am fearfully and wonderfully made. My substance was not hid from you when I was made in secret and I was curiously wrought in the lowest parts of the Earth. You saw my substance yet being imperfect, and all my members were written in your book.

How precious are your thoughts unto me, O God. How great is the sum of them. It thrills me to realize that every morning when I awaken you are still with me. Search me, O God, and know my heart. Try me, and know my thoughts. See if there be any wicked way in me, and lead me in your everlasting way. In Jesus' name I pray, Amen.

11. PAUL'S PRAYER FOR SPIRITUAL UNDERSTANDING

That the God of our Lord Jesus Christ, the Father of glory, may give unto you the spirit of wisdom and revelation in the knowledge of him: the eyes of your understanding being enlightened; that ye may know what is the hope of his calling, and what the riches of the glory of his inheritance in the saints, and what is the exceeding greatness of his power to usward who believe, according to the working of his mighty power, which he wrought in Christ, when he raised him from the dead, and set him at his own right hand in the heavenly places, far above all principality, and power, and might, and dominion, and every name that is named, not only in this world, but also in that which is to come: And hath put all things under his feet, and gave him to be the head over all things to the church, which is his body, the fullness of him that filleth all.

(EPHESIANS 1: 17-23)

In this prayer we see Paul praying for the Ephesians, that they would become wise in the knowledge of the Lord Jesus Christ. He asks that God would open their eyes and enlighten them, that they would know the hope of His calling and the riches of the glory of His inheritance in the saints, and he wants the people to know the exceeding greatness of God's power.

He praises God for all things, including the working of His mighty power in those of us who believe. He cites the importance of belief—a belief that transcends anything this world has to offer. Because God raised Jesus from the dead, that same resurrection power is now available to us. Jesus now sits at the right hand of God in the heavenly places, and He is the head of the Church, which is the fullness of Him.

The Personalized Prayer of Paul for Spiritual Understanding

Abba-Father, you are the God of the Lord Jesus Christ and the Father of glory. I ask you to give me the spirit of wisdom and revelation in the knowledge of Jesus. May the eyes of my understanding be enlightened by you so that I may fully comprehend the hope of your calling in my life. Help me to fully realize what the riches of my spiritual inheritance are.

I ask, also, that you would help me to know and experience the exceeding greatness of your power as I place my faith and trust in you. Thank you for the working of your mighty power in my life through Jesus Christ. Thank you for raising Him from the dead and setting Him at your own right hand in the heavenly places, far above all principality, power, might, dominion, and every name that is named on Earth and in Heaven.

I praise you for putting all things under His feet. I thank you that He is the head over all things in the Church, which is the Body of Christ. It is so wonderful to know that His fullness fills all in all. In Jesus' name I pray, Amen.

In this chapter I've cited only eleven prayers that are found in the Bible, but there are so many more. The Book of Psalms, for example, is filled with the personal prayers of David and others. Here are some additional ones that you may wish to personalize in your own devotional life:

- John 17
- Habakkuk 3:2-19
- Ezra 9:5-15
- Daniel 9:4-19
- Isaiah 38:2-8
- 2 Kings 19:15-19
- 2 Samuel 7:18-29
- Genesis 18:23-25
- Acts 7:59-60
- Exodus 32:9-14
- Nehemiah 1:1-2:9
- Luke 22:35-46

In your personal study of the Bible, I hope you will look for other prayers and learn to personalize each one. In this way you will experience the power of God's Word, and this will change your life.

Beth Moore wrote, "There are parts of our calling, works of the Holy Spirit, and defeats of the darkness that will come no other way than through furious, fervent, faith-filled, unceasing prayer."

PART III

From Glory to Glory He's Changing Me

From glory to glory He's changing me,
changing me, changing me.
His likeness and image to perfect in me,
the love of God shown to the world.

CHANGE CAN BE GOOD

The above verse is from a hymn we used to sing in church. It reveals how God is constantly at work behind the scenes in our lives to change us, mold us, shape us, and transform us into the image of His Son. Our God is an active God, and He wants us to be open to His dynamics in every area of our lives.

It is based on this Bible verse: "But we all, with open face beholding as in a glass the glory of the Lord, are changed into the same image from glory to glory, even as by the Spirit of the Lord" (2 Corinthians 3:18).

Yes, God is changing you from glory to glory. Paul wrote, "For we are his workmanship, created in Christ Jesus unto good works, which God hath before ordained that we should walk in them" (Ephesians 2:10). You and I are works in progress, and He will never be finished with us.

God is the potter; we are the clay, and He, the Master Potter, is constantly at work at His wheel molding, shaping, and changing us. He is an expert and He knows what He is doing. "But now, O Lord, thou art our father; we are the clay, and thou our potter; and we are all the work of thy hand" (Isaiah 64:8). The work of the potter is to shape and form the vessel until it becomes a work of art and a practical object for service. The changes you are going through are a part of His process in your life. You are His work of art, and He is designing you to change in ways that will help you to be practical in His service.

Change is a big part of life, and accepting certain changes is one of the biggest challenges you will ever face. However, it is vitally important that we remain open to the changes God wants to bring about in our lives. He is helping us to become more like Jesus. In fact, this is His goal for us.

When things are not going well in your life, do you pray, "Lord, please change these circumstances" or do you pray, "Lord, please change me!"? The second prayer is the better one, because it shows that you understand that whatever comes your way is a part of God's plan for you. Keep in mind that every person you meet is your teacher and that every circumstance is helping to shape and mold you into Jesus' image.

While many people would like to change things on the outside of their lives or their bodies, God is at work on the inside. He is far less concerned about external appearances than you are. He cares about the condition of your heart/spirit. "For the Lord seeth not as man seeth; for man looketh on the outward appearance, but the Lord looketh on the heart" (1 Samuel 16:7).

God, our Father and our potter, is at work on our hearts. He wants our hearts to be moved with the same things that move His heart, to be broken with the same things that break His heart. He wants to cleanse our hearts and make them pure.

Yes, God is both our Father and our potter. We should never strive with our Father who is our Potter by complaining, "Why have you let this happen to me?" God knows what He is doing: "And we know that all things work together for good to them that love God, to them who are the called according to his purpose" (Romans 8:28). If we believe this verse, we must accept everything that happens as a part of God's will for our lives.

Every change that we experience is a fresh way to experience God's glory. What is God's glory? It is His radiant beauty and splendor. It is a taste of Heaven on Earth. It is His magnificence. When we look to Him during the experiences of life, we become radiated by His power and His love, and this enables us to accept the changes that are taking place.

David wrote, "I sought the Lord, and he heard me, and delivered me from all my fears. They looked unto him, and were lightened [radiant]: and their faces were not ashamed" (Psalm 34:5). When we look to the Lord, we see His glory and we experience it first-hand.

When we pray His Word, we are changed.

FROM GLORY TO GLORY HE'S CHANGING ME

Glory involves strength, magnificence, splendor, majesty, and greatness. To have glory is to be of great value and importance. Paul said that we are made in the image and glory of God. As we study the word "glory" in the Bible, we see that it has several connotations, but one of these clearly is strength. "The glory of young men is their strength" (Proverbs 20:29).

We possess an inherent glory that comes from being made in God's image—a very glorious image indeed. God's glory is being revealed to us through the sufferings and changes we go through. We are partaking of His glory now, and at some future time we will experience His glory fully, as Paul wrote: "For I reckon that the sufferings of this present time are not worthy to be compared with the glory which shall be revealed in us" (Romans 8:18).

Ralph Waldo Emerson wrote, "Our greatest glory is not in never failing but in rising up every time we fail." Yes, this is the essence of glory—the strength to keep on keeping on. It is this that brings about change in our lives.

Yes, from glory to glory He's changing us, and praying God's Word helps us to understand what He is doing in our lives as changes occur. Graham Cooke wrote, "Prayer is the art of speaking God's Word back to Him. That's why we are learning to pray with God, not towards Him. We're learning to pray with the answer, not to try and find one."

Now there's a change in perspective—to pray with God, not towards Him. It is praying with the answers in mind, not trying to find answers. The answers are already available in His Word, and if we use His Word as our most important prayer resource, we will know what His answers are.

Such prayer leads us into the glory of God. Isn't it wonderful to know that God shares His glory with us? When we receive His gifts as we pray we are receiving His glory into our own lives. His glory reflects His essential nature, and He wants us to partake of His nature. The promises of God's Word help us to see that He wants us to glory in Him, to partake of His glory, and to share His glory with others.

One of those promises says, "Whereby are given unto us exceeding great and precious promises: that by these ye might be partakers of the divine nature, having escaped the corruption that is in the world through lust" (2 Peter 1:4).

FROM STRENGTH TO STRENGTH HE'S CHANGING ME

As we have pointed out, one interpretation of the word "glory" is strength, and the Bible is replete in its examples of how God wants us to receive and experience His strength. Warren Wiersbe wrote, "The remedy for discouragement is the Word of God. When you feed your heart and mind with its truth, you regain your perspective and find renewed strength."

The Psalmist wrote, "They go from strength to strength" (Psalm 84:7). Like the Hebrews of old, we can go from strength to strength if we determine in our hearts to follow Him.

I believe you will gain strength as you pray the prayers within this book. They are based on the Bible, and praying God's Word is a great way to feed your heart and mind with the His truths. This is a life-changing experience, and it takes us from glory to glory and from strength to strength. The Bible has much to tell us about strength, and the following are some key verses:

- "I can do all things through Christ which strengtheneth me" (Philippians 4:13).
- "He giveth power to the faint; and to them that have no might he increaseth strength" (Isaiah 40:29).
- "My soul melteth for heaviness: strengthen thou me according unto thy word" (Psalm 119:28).
- "Finally, my brethren be strong in the Lord, and in the power of his might" (Ephesians 6:10).

- "But they that wait upon the Lord shall renew their strength; they shall mount up with wings as eagles; they shall run, and not be weary; and they shall walk, and not faint" (Isaiah 40:31).
- "And he said unto me, My grace is sufficient for thee: for my strength is made perfect in weakness. Most gladly therefore will I rather glory in my infirmities, that the power of Christ may rest upon me" (2 Corinthians 12:9).
- "God is our refuge and strength, a very present help in trouble" (Psalm 46:1).
- "The joy of the Lord is your strength" (Nehemiah 8:10).
- "But be not thou far from me, O Lord: O my strength, haste thou to help me" (Psalm 22:19).
- "The Lord is my strength and my shield; my heart trusted in him, and I am helped: therefore my heart greatly rejoiceth; and with my song will I praise him" (Psalm 28:7).
- "The Lord is my strength and my song, and is become my salvation" (Psalm 118:14).
- "That he would grant you, according to the riches of his glory, to be strengthened with might by his Spirit in the inner man" (Ephesians 3:16).

The above are but a few of the many verses about strength in the Bible. From these we learn that God is our strength, that He strengthens us, increases our strength, and imparts His strength to us. Note that He strengthens us according to His Word, His strength is made perfect in our weakness, and by experiencing His joy we find strength.

All of these blessings are ours when we learn to pray His Word. Yes, from strength to strength He's changing us. Andrew Murray wrote, "Do not strive in your own strength, cast yourself at the feet of the Lord Jesus, and wait upon Him in the sure confidence that He is with you and works in you. Strive in prayer; let faith fill your heart—so you will be strong in the Lord, and in the power of His might."

FROM DEATH TO LIFE
HE'S CHANGING ME

As we pray God's Word, new life is imparted to us— life from His living Word—and everything about us becomes new. Paul wrote, "For the law of the Spirit of life in Christ Jesus hath made me free from the law of sin and death" (Romans 8:2).

Carnal-mindedness leads to death, but spiritual-mindedness is life and peace. (See Romans 8:6.) Our minds are transformed when we pray God's Word and this leads us to life and peace. Christianity is "the land of new beginnings."

Yes, Jesus raises us from spiritual death. He is the only one who can, because He is God incarnate. He arose from the dead. He is life and He came to give us a more abundant life. (See John 10:10.) When a person is spiritually dead (i.e. without Jesus) he or she is unknowingly alienated from God.

We need to be born again, as Jesus said to Nicodemus, "Verily, verily, I say unto thee, except a man be born again, he cannot see the kingdom of God" (John 3:3). We are born in sin, and that's why we need to be born again. The Bible says, "For if you live according to the sinful nature, you will die; but if by the Spirit you put to death the misdeeds of the body, you will live" (Romans 8:1).

The choice, then, is a simple one: life or death? We can go from spiritual death to resurrection power if we understand that God wants to give us new life. "Therefore, if any man be in Christ, he is a new creature: old things are passed away; behold, all things are become new" (2 Corinthians 5:17).

God wants to bring new life to you, and through His Son and His Word you will receive it. The Christian life is one of constant renewal and change. Oswald Chambers wrote, "All of God's people are ordinary people who have been made extraordinary by the purpose He has given them."

The God who made us wants to remake us into the image of His Son. Let Him renew your mind as you pray His Word.

FROM DARKNESS TO LIGHT
HE'S CHANGING ME

We live in a very dark world. God wants us to be His lights in this dark world. The Bible says, "Giving thanks unto the Father, which hath made us meet to be partakers of the inheritance of the saints in light: who hath delivered us from the power of darkness, and hath translated us into the kingdom of his dear Son" (Colossians 1:12-13).

Step out of the darkness and let the light of the Lord Jesus flood your being. "But ye are a chosen generation, a royal priesthood, a holy nation, a peculiar people; that ye should shew forth the praises of him who hath called you out of darkness into his marvelous light" (1 Peter 2:9).

Darkness brings gloom into people's hearts, whereas light brings joy. Live in the marvelous light of Jesus Christ. Francis Bacon wrote, "In order for the light to shine so brightly, the darkness must be present." This relates to John 1:4-5: "In him was life; and the life was the light of men. And the light shineth in darkness; and the darkness comprehended it not."

One little candle can bring light to a dark room; its tiny light dispels the darkness. As we study God's Word and pray its truths, light comes to us and we are filled with light. We need to let our light shine in the darkness. As we do so, the darkness will be dispelled and the truth will prevail.

The Psalmist wrote, "Thy word is a lamp unto my feet, and a light unto my path." Let the light of God's Word lead you and guide you. You can walk in the light of God's Word and His love. John wrote, "This is the message that we have heard of him, and declare unto you, that God is light, and in him is no darkness at all. If we say that we have fellowship with him, and walk in darkness, we lie, and do not the truth: But if we walk in the light as he is in the light, we have fellowship one with another, and the blood of Jesus Christ his Son cleanseth us from all sin" (1 John 1:5-70).

Light has many properties and two of the most important are that it cleanses and purifies. God, who is light, wants to cleanse and purify your heart as you walk out of the darkness into His marvelous light. Keep on walking toward the light and let the light of His truth shine in you and through you.

As we learn to live and walk in the light, we will lead many people to Jesus. So many around us are living in darkness, gloom, and despair. Let them know about the Light of the world who is Jesus. Dwight L. Moody wrote, "We are told to let our light shine, and if it does, we won't need to tell anybody it does. Lighthouses don't fire cannons to call attention to their shining—they just shine."

FROM FEAR TO LOVE HE'S CHANGING ME

Darkness leads to fear, and fear is a condition that brings about great turmoil, confusion, and torment. There is a sure way to avoid fear, and that is through God's love. The more we experience the love of God personally, the more we are able to let our light shine. We can walk through this world of darkness without any fear.

Faith expressing itself through love will conquer fear. The Apostle John wrote, "There is no fear in love; but perfect love casteth out fear: because fear hath torment. He that feareth is not made perfect in love" (1 John 4:18). God is love. As we walk with Him, we experience His love, and this is enough. Knowing that He is with us and that He will not let us face life's challenges alone takes away the fear.

Zac Poonen wrote, "If you fear God, you really need fear nothing else." Fear, worry, and anxiety are tools of the devil that are designed to weaken our faith. They really have no place in our lives. As God moves us from fear to love, we notice that anxiety and worry vanish. The Bible says, "Yea, though I walk through the valley of the shadow of death, I will fear no evil: for thou art with me" (Psalm 23:4). The devil and his darkness—all his dread thoughts of doom and horror—cannot touch us when we are in the Lord's presence.

"Are you facing fear today? Perhaps you are afraid of losing your job, of developing cancer or being left by your spouse. At times all of us experience fear. But don't allow fear to keep you from being used by God. He has kept you thus far; trust Him for the rest of the way" (A.W. Tozer).

FROM GLOOM TO JOY HE'S CHANGING ME

Gloominess brings the darkness of the world into your own soul. This is not God's will for you. He wants you to be joyful and triumphant. Indeed, His joy is your strength. (See Nehemiah 8:10.)You can find joy in life's journey if you will walk away from the darkness and gloom all around you.

Never forget that, as Tielhard de Chardin wrote, "You are not a human being in search of a spiritual experience. You are a spiritual being immersed in a human experience."

What is Christian joy? It is far more than a feeling. It is a state of being. As you walk in the joy of the Lord, your life will change completely. The expressions on your face will change. Your words will change into positive declarations. You will walk with greater confidence and strength.

While some forms of religion may be gloomy, real Christianity is full of joy. To be filled with God is to be filled with joy. When people see your joy, they will want it for themselves, and they will wonder where it comes from because it is such a rare quality. When that happens you will be able to share the gospel with them.

It is possible to be joyful even in the midst of suffering if we are living in God's presence. Theophane Venard wrote, "Be merry, really merry. The life of a true Christian should be a perpetual jubilee." Joy is a choice you can make each morning.

Praying God's Word should be a joyful experience for you. I encourage you to do so each day.

FROM EARTHLY THINGS TO THE HEAVENLY

The things of this earth are temporal. They may hold some appeal, but it is not a lasting appeal. Paul wrote, "While we look not at the things which are seen: for the things which are seen are temporal; but the things which are not seen are eternal" (2 Corinthians 4:18).

The Word of God states, "Love not the world, neither the things that are in the world. If any man love the world, the love of the Father is not in him. For all that is in the world, the lust of the flesh, and the lust of the eyes, and the pride of life, is not of the Father, but of the world. And the world passeth away, and the lust thereof: but he that doeth the will of God abideth forever" (1 John 2:15-17).

Worldliness and carnality are to be avoided at all costs. The lure of this world is empty and meaningless, but the lure of eternity is filled with so many good things. Arthur Schopenhauer wrote, "Almost all of our sorrows spring out of our relations with other people. There is no more mistaken path to happiness than worldliness."

If we are going to be the salt of the Earth and the light of the world, we must walk in purity. We are in this world, but we are not of it. We are ambassadors from a different kingdom. We are princes and princesses in God's royal family. The way to get out of worldliness is to seek God's holiness. It is then that we know we will be leaving earthly things behind.

Jesus said, "Lay not up for yourselves treasures upon earth, where moth and rust doth corrupt, and where thieves break through and steal: But lay up for yourselves treasures in heaven, where neither moth nor rust doth corrupt, and where thieves do not break through and steal. For where your treasure is, there will your heart be also" (Matthew 6:19-21).

HIS LIKENESS AND IMAGE WILL BE PERFECTED IN ME

God wants the likeness and image of Jesus to be perfected in us. He already sees us through Jesus' eyes. Jesus abides within us, and we abide in Him. As we get closer to Him through praying His Word, we will become more like Him, and everything about us will change.

God's Word and His ministers are at work in our lives to perfect us, as Paul wrote: "For the perfecting of the saints, for the work of ministry, for the edifying of the body of Christ: Till we all come in the unity of the faith, and of the knowledge of the Son of God, unto a perfect man, unto the measure of the stature of the fullness of Christ" (Ephesians 5:12-14).

The Father is at work in our lives to conform us into the image of His Son. This happens as we draw close to Him and grow in the knowledge of the Lord Jesus Christ. Praying God's Word helps us in this process.

We must know who Jesus is and what He has done and is doing. We must know His Word and walk according to His will. Though this process may be gradual, we know it is God's will for us. We are predestined to be conformed to the image of the Son of God. (See Romans 8:29).

Becoming Christ-like is God's work in our lives, and He will accomplish it. "Being confident of this very thing, that he which hath begun a good work in you will perform it until the day of Jesus Christ" (Philippians 1:6).

CONSTRUCTION ZONE AHEAD—DRIVE SLOWLY

Are there things in your life that you would like to have changed? Would you like to change your thoughts, your speech, your health, your motives, your attitudes, your perspective, or your relationships?

You and I are works in progress. The Master Architect has a goal in mind for us. Michelangelo looked at a huge block of marble. Though beautiful, it was unfinished. He began to chisel that giant marble into the image he saw with his mind's eye— the magnificent statue of David.

This sculpture is seventeen feet tall, one of the greatest masterpieces ever created by man. It is glorious in its beauty and magnificence. However, it took Michelangelo many years to produce this majestic work of art. How did he accomplish this? He said, "In every block of marble I see a statue as plain as though it stood before me, shaped and perfect in attitude and action. I have only to hew away the rough walls that imprison the lovely apparition to reveal it to other eyes as mine see it."

That is what God is doing in our lives right now. He is molding and shaping us into the image He already sees. That's why we must cooperate with Him and not ever resist Him. Don't question what He is doing, but trust (and know) that what He is doing is right.

God is not finished with you yet. However, for Him to complete the work that He has begun in your life, you must surrender your life to Him. In every part of your life He must increase and you must decrease. Paul wrote, "I am crucified with Christ: nevertheless, I live; yet not I, but Christ liveth in me; and the life which I now live in the flesh I live by the faith of the Son of God, who loved me, and gave himself for me" (Galatians 2:20).

Following Jesus means that we must walk away from sin, become obedient disciples, and put Him first in our lives. We must let the power of God's Holy Spirit do its work in us. "Now unto him that is able to do exceeding abundantly above all that we ask or think, according to the power that worketh in us" (Ephesians 3:20) God's power is at work in our lives, and it is important for us to go with His flow instead of trying to do things in our own power.

John prophesied, "Beloved, now are we the sons of God, and it doth not yet appear what we shall be: but we know that, when he shall appear, we shall be like him; for we shall see him as he is. And every man that hath this hope in him purifieth himself, even as he is pure" (1 John 3:2-3).

"For we are his workmanship. . . "(Ephesians 2:10). God is the Master Architect and His work is perfect. You are not an accident. God has a purpose and a plan for your life. Jeremiah wrote, "For I know the thoughts that I think toward you, saith the Lord, thoughts of peace, and not of evil, to give you an expected end" (Jeremiah 29:11). What is that expected end? That you be conformed to the image of Jesus Christ.

C.S. Lewis wrote, "God became man to turn creatures into sons: not simply to produce better men of the old kind but to produce a new kind of man." Newness of life is yours every day of your life. All you have to do is receive it.

When God created you, He created you in His image, and He now wants to restore you; He wants to have His likeness and image perfected in you, and this will result in His love being shown to the whole world. As Corrie ten Boom wrote, "Never be afraid to trust an unknown future to a known God."

Praying God's Word changes things. Most importantly it changes you. May you be changed from glory to glory and from strength to strength as you pray the prayers within this book.

PART IV

Principles of Prayer

Oswald Smith wrote, "When we work, we work; when we pray, God works." How true this is, and this is one principle of prayer. God is always at work in our behalf and, as we speak to Him in prayer, we are able to grasp this truth more fully and we even see what He is doing for us.

A RELATIONSHIP WITH GOD

Our Father wants to have fellowship with us. This is one of the reasons why He created us, so that we would know Him and enjoy Him forever. He loves to have intimate communion with His children in the same way that most earthly fathers delight in spending time with their children.

Relating to God involves dialogue, and the word dialogue connotes a two-way conversation. It is through persistent prayer that we are able to discern God's voice speaking to us. Of course, we must take time, as we're praying, to listen for His voice. Jesus said, "My sheep hear my voice, and I know them, and they follow me" (John 10:27). Do you recognize His voice when He is speaking to you?

It would appear that most people do not listen carefully when someone is speaking to them. God is speaking to us all the time, and paying attention to Him is vitally important to our spiritual growth and development. Of course, He loves to hear us speaking to Him, and He always takes time to listen. He wants to be there for us.

Our heavenly Father has adopted us into His family, and we are His children. As we come to Him in prayer, we can imagine an intimate relationship with Him that is akin to a child sitting on his father's lap. I remember when I used to hold my sons on my lap while reading to them. Those are some precious memories and they were times of intimacy, warmth, and closeness.

Prayer is so much more than asking our Father to do things for us or to give things to us. It is fellowship of the highest kind and it is so meaningful. Through this fellowship we learn what God has in store for us and what He wants from us. We experience the depth of His everlasting love for us.

So, one of the principles of prayer involves strengthening our relationship with God. "The purpose of prayer is not to receive what you asked for, but to strengthen your relationship with God" (Author unknown).

RECOGNIZING AND ADORING GOD

Our Father loves to hear us tell Him that we love Him. This truly is music to His ears. We adore Him because we know who He is, and it is this recognition that makes us want to pray. Jesus, in the Lord's Prayer, began with adoration of our heavenly Father and we should too.

We thank God for what He does for us, but we adore Him for who He is—our Creator, Almighty God, our heavenly Father, and our Guide unto death. (See Psalm 48:14.) He is our God forever, the mighty God, our refuge and strength.

All these attributes of God make us want to adore Him and to express our adoration to Him. To adore is to worship, love, and to pay homage to. Our Father is worthy of our adoration at all times.

Prayer can lead us into worship, which involves humbling ourselves before God. Through worship we get to know Him, and we are able to experience His presence where we find fullness of joy and pleasures forevermore. (See Psalm 16:11.)

Do you pray with adoration? C.S. Lewis wrote, "We only learn to behave ourselves in the presence of God." If his words are true, and I believe they are, we need to remain in His presence, for this will result in walking in love and obedience.

CONFESSION OF SIN

Another principle of prayer is that it enables us to confess our sins to God who already knows everything about us. If this is true, then, why do we need to pray? It is simply because our Father knows that confession will restore us to a close relationship with Him—His highest goal for us.

Confession will also bring spiritual freedom to us, and this will improve our outlook, our attitude, and our sense of purpose. It will enable us to walk in the light as God is in the light. John wrote, "If we say that we have fellowship with him [God], and walk in darkness [sin], we lie and do not the truth: But if we walk in the light, as he is in the light, we have fellowship with one another, and the blood of Jesus Christ cleanseth us from all sin. . .. If we confess our sins, he is faithful and just to forgive us our sins, and to cleanse us from all unrighteousness" (1 John 1:3-9).

Sin separates us from God. I believe it breaks His heart when He sees one of His children sin. How wonderful it is that He has given us the means to find spiritual restoration through confession of sin, which frees us from the guilt of the past and the fear of the future.

A.W. Pink wrote, "Prayer is not appointed for the furnishing of God with the knowledge of what we need, but it is designed as a confession to Him of our sense of the need. In this, as in everything, God's thoughts are not ours. God requires that His gifts should be sought for. He designs to be honored by our asking, just as He is to be thanked by us after He has bestowed His blessing."

When we confess our sins to God, we need to be specific and we need to be repentant. True repentance is shown by godly sorrow—the kind of sorrow that comes from God as a gift to us. His goodness leads us to repentance. (See 2 Corinthians 7:10 and Romans 2:4.)

SUPPLICATION

Another principle of prayer is supplication, which means to ask for something in great humility and earnest expectation. It is a form of request that we use when we have need of something. If we base our requests on God's promises, we can be sure that He hears us and that He will meet the need. (See 1 John 5:14-15). We must pray according to His will, and we must pray in Jesus' name.

Jesus said, "Ask, and it shall be given you; seek, and ye shall find; knock, and it shall be opened unto you" (Matthew 7:7). The Father knows what you have need of, but He wants you to come to Him in humility to ask Him for it.

I might know that my child or grandchild wants something, but unless he or she comes to me and asks me for it, I may not act upon their wish immediately. God, our heavenly Father, makes this wonderful promise to His children: "But my God shall supply all your need according to his riches in glory by Christ Jesus" (Philippians 4:19).

There is, of course, a big difference between wants and needs. As Abraham Maslow pointed out in his Hierarchy of Needs, the greatest need of the human soul is union with God, and the Father is ready to meet this need as you draw near to Him. I believe that from this union all other needs will be met automatically.

Jesus said, "But seek ye first the kingdom of God, and his righteousness; and all these things will be added unto you" (Matthew 6:33). This is an amazing promise to you from your Father in Heaven—further evidence of the depth of His love for you.

Thomas Brooks wrote, "If any prayer be a duty, then secret prayer must be superlatively so, for it prepares and fits the soul for all other supplication."

Do you have needs that you want God to meet? Take them to Him in prayer. He always listens and He want to meet your needs.

PERSEVERANCE AND DILIGENCE

Andrew Murray wrote, "Blessed is the one who is not staggered by God's delay or silence or apparent refusal, but is strong in faith, giving glory to God. Such faith perseveres, persistently, if need be, and will not fail to inherit the blessing."

Persistent, prevailing prayer that is uttered by a diligent believer will be heard and answered. James wrote, "The effectual fervent prayer of a righteous man availeth much" (James 5:16). We don't use the word avail much these days, but it simply means "effective use or help." The effective prayer of faith brings results, but we must persevere. We must pray without ceasing. We must not give up.

What God promises to us He will do. "For all the promises of God in him are yea, and in him Amen, unto the glory of God by us" (2 Corinthians 1:20). All God's promises are answered with yes and amen. Why? Because His answers bring glory to Him.

In the Gospel of Luke we read about a widow who went to a judge for help against her adversary. She went to the judge several times until he finally heard her and granted her plea. This is a great example of persistence, the kind of persistence we need to demonstrate in prayer.

This is strong faith, and, as Andrew Murray said above, it ". . . will not fail to inherit the blessing."

THANKSGIVING, REJOICING, AND PRAISE

Another great principle of prayer is joyful thanksgiving that results in praise to God. Paul wrote, "Rejoice evermore. Pray without ceasing. In everything give thanks: for this is the will of God in Christ Jesus concerning you" (1 Thessalonians 5:16-18).

The prayer of thanksgiving gives joy to the one praying and to God himself. The above verse tells us that giving thanks is God's will for us. Seldom in the Scriptures does God spell out His will as clearly and specifically as He does here.

Why does He want us to be thankful? Why does He want us to praise Him? It's not just because He loves to hear our praise. He wants us to praise Him because He knows this will bring great joy to us. A happy soul rejoices.

Never forget that "The joy of the Lord is your strength" (Nehemiah 8:10). As you receive answers to your prayers, you experience His joy. It is ". . . joy unspeakable and full of glory" (1 Peter 1:8).

So, "Let us thank God heartily as often as we pray that we have His Spirit in us to teach us to pray. Thanksgiving will draw our hearts out to God and keep us engaged with Him; it will take our attention from ourselves and give the Spirit room in our hearts" (Andrew Murray).

In this chapter we have covered six important principles of prayer:

1. A relationship with God
2. Recognizing and adoring God
3. Confession of sin
4. Supplication
5. Perseverance and diligence
6. Thanksgiving, rejoicing, and praise

These are all vital components of effective prayer, and there are many more. Let me simply list some of them below:

- Praying in Jesus' name
- A consciousness of our need before God
- Believing in God's willingness to meet our need
- Claiming His promises as we pray
- Faith
- Humility
- Passion
- Praying in harmony with God's will

I have not elaborated upon the above list because each principle has been discussed before. Many of these principles are also elucidated in the prayers to follow. These are truly *Prayers That Change Things*; they are prayers that will change you. So, believe and receive as you pray.

PART V

Thoughts About Prayer

The following quotations are from well-known authors, leaders, and teachers. Their thoughts about prayer will help us see how important prayer actually is.

"I have been driven many times upon my knees by the overwhelming conviction that I had nowhere else to go. My own wisdom and that of all about me seemed insufficient for that day" (Abraham Lincoln).

"The more you pray, the less you'll panic. The more you worship, the less you worry. You'll feel more patient and less pressured" (Rick Warren).

"In prayer it is better to have a heart without words than words without a heart" (John Bunyan).

"We tend to use prayer as a last resort, but God wants it to be our first line of defense. We pray when there's nothing else we can do, but God wants us to pray before we do anything at all. Most of us would prefer, however, to spend our time doing something that will

get immediate results. We don't want to wait for God to resolve matters in His good time because His idea of 'a good time' is seldom in sync with ours" (Oswald Chambers).

"Is prayer your steering wheel or your spare tire?" (Corrie ten Boom).

"Prayer may just be the most powerful tool mankind has" (Ted Dekker).

"I have so much to do that I shall spend the first three hours in prayer" (Martin Luther).

"Sometimes I go to God and say, 'God, if thou dost never answer another prayer while I live on this earth, I will still worship thee as long as I live and in the ages to come for what thou hast done already.' God's already put me so far in debt that if I were to live one million millenniums I couldn't pay Him for what He's done for me" (A.W. Tozer).

"Those blessings are sweetest that are won with prayer and worn with thanks" (Thomas Goodwin).

"He who kneels the most, stands the best" (Dwight L. Moody).

"Your prayer for someone may or may not change them, but it always changes YOU" (Craig Groeschel).

"For me, prayer is a surge of the heart; it is a simple look turned toward Heaven, it is a cry of recognition and of love, embracing both trial and joy" (Therese de Lisieux).

"We never know how God will answer our prayers, but

we can expect that He will get us involved in His plan for the answer. If we are true intercessors, we must be ready to take part in God's work on behalf of the people for whom we pray" (Corrie ten Boom).

"We should seek not so much to pray but to become prayer" (Francis of Assisi).

"Prayer is beyond any question the highest activity of the human soul. Man is at his greatest and highest when upon his knees he comes face to face with God" (D. Martyn Lloyd-Jones).

"Each time, before you intercede, be quiet first, and worship God in His glory. Think of what He can do, and how He delights to hear the prayers of His redeemed people. Think of your place and privilege in Christ, and expect great things!" (Andrew Murray).

"Answered prayer is the interchange of love between the Father and His child" (Andrew Murray).

"As we come to grips with our own selfishness and stupidity, we make friends with the impostor and accept that we are impoverished and broken and realize that, if we were not, we would be God. The art of gentleness toward ourselves leads to being gentle with others—and is a natural prerequisite for our presence to God in prayer" (Brennan Manning).

"When I pray for another person, I am praying for God to open my eyes so that I can see that person as God does, and then enter into the stream of love that God already directs toward that person" (Phillip Yancey).

"Prayer is not overcoming God's reluctance. It is

laying hold of His willingness" (Martin Luther).

"We can be tired, weary and emotionally distraught, but after spending time alone with God, we find that He injects into our bodies energy, power and strength" (Charles Stanley).

"The goal of prayer is to live all of my life and speak all of my words in the joyful awareness of the presence of God. Prayer becomes real when we grasp the reality and goodness of God's constant presence with 'the real me.' Jesus lived His everyday life in conscious awareness of His Father" (John Ortberg, Jr.).

"No one can believe how powerful prayer is and what it can effect, except those who have learned it by experience. Whenever I have prayed earnestly, I have been heard and have obtained more than I prayed for. God sometimes delays, but He always comes" (Martin Luther).

"Praying and sinning will never live together in the same heart. Prayer will consume sin, or sin will choke prayer" (J.C. Ryle).

"The sooner I learn to forget myself in the desire that He may be glorified, the richer will be the blessing that prayer will bring to myself. No one ever loses by what he sacrifices to the Father" (Andrew Murray).

"We do not want to be beginners [at prayer], but let us be convinced of the fact that we will never be anything but beginners all our life" (Thomas Merton).

"Prayer is the most powerful resource we have in this life; yet, many only turn to it as a last resort. When unbelievers pray for repentance of sin and ask for God's forgiveness, prayer is the spiritual dynamite that obliterates the darkness and despair of a sin-soaked soul" (Franklin Graham).

"A man may study because his brain is hungry for knowledge, even Bible knowledge, but he prays because his soul is hungry for God" (Leonard Ravenhill).

"Remember, He WANTS your fellowship, and He has done everything possible to make it a reality. He has forgiven your sins, at the cost of His own dear Son. He has given you His Word, and the priceless privilege of prayer and worship" (Billy Graham).

"Don't forget to pray today because God did not forget to wake you up this morning" (Oswald Chambers).

"If we seem to get no good by attempting to draw near to Him, we may be sure we will get none by keeping away from Him" (John Newton).

"Prayer does change things, all kinds of things. But the most important thing it changes is us. As we engage in this communion with God more deeply and come to know the One with whom we are speaking more intimately, that growing knowledge of God reveals to us all the more brilliantly who we are and our need to change in conformity to Him. Prayer changes us profoundly" (R.C. Sproul).

"The ministry of prayer, if it be anything worthy of the name, is a ministry of ardor, a ministry of unwearied and intense longing after God" (E.M. Bounds).

"Men may spurn our appeals, reject our message, oppose our arguments, despise our persons, but they are helpless against our prayers" (J. Sidlow Baxter).

"I believe God has heard my prayers. He will make it manifest in His own good time that He has heard me. I have recorded my petitions that when God has answered them, His name will be glorified" (George Mueller).

"Work as if everything depended upon work and pray as if everything depended upon prayer" (William Booth).

"Prayer without study would be empty. Study without prayer would be blind" (Karl Barth).

PART VI

Word Prayers About Your Feelings and Conditions

1

Absent-Mindedness

Now we beseech you, brethren, by the coming of our Lord Jesus Christ, and by our gathering unto him, that ye be not soon shaken in mind, or be troubled, neither by spirit, nor by word, nor by letter as from us, as that the day of Christ is at hand.

(2 THESSALONIANS 2:1-2)

Central Focus: Keep your mind stayed on the Lord. By keeping Him as your focus, you will become more mentally focused and less absent-minded.

Prayer: Dear Father, thank you for helping me overcome all absent-mindedness by staying focused on you and your Word. Through your grace, I will be renewed in the spirit of my mind. Thank you for giving me the mind of Christ, which is always focused and never absent-minded.

By your mercies, I now present my body as a living sacrifice, which is holy and acceptable unto you. I realize that this is my reasonable service unto you. I choose not to be conformed to this world any longer. Instead, I will be transformed by the renewing of my mind, that I may prove what is your good, acceptable, and perfect will.

Father, keep me from all carnal-mindedness as I endeavor to follow your will in all things, for I realize that carnal-mindedness leads to death, but spiritual-mindedness leads to life and peace. I will walk in peace of mind, as you lead me each step of the way.

Thank you, Father, for your promise to keep me in perfect peace when my mind is stayed on you. I trust you completely to free me from all absent-mindedness. I will trust you forever, for you are my everlasting strength.

With your help, I will love you with all my heart, soul, strength, and mind. This will enable me to love my neighbor as myself. Thank you for your great love for me, Father. Because you love me, I am able to love you, others, and myself. Hallelujah!

Thank you, Lord, for all the promises of your Word. I now renounce all absent-mindedness, carnal mindedness, and double-mindedness. I choose mental stability for myself, for I know that a double-minded person is unstable in all his ways.

I praise you for helping me to be Christ-minded. Because of your grace, I know I now have His mind—a mind that is filled with love, peace, and joy.

In Jesus' powerful name I pray, Amen.

Scriptures: Ephesians 4:23; Romans 12:1-2; Romans 8:6; Isaiah 26:3-4; Luke 10:27; 1 John 4:19; James 1:8; 1 Corinthians 2:16.

Personal Affirmation: From this day forward I will walk purposefully, remaining focused on the Lord, living in His presence, and keeping mindful of the will of God. I choose to put all absent-mindedness behind me and to go forth with an attitude of spiritual mindedness.

Reflection: *"We must do our business faithfully, without trouble or disquiet, recalling our mind to God mildly, and with tranquility, as often as we find it wandering from him"* (Brother Lawrence).

2

An Arrogant Attitude

The fear of the Lord is to hate evil: pride, and arrogancy, and the evil way, and the forward mouth do I hate.

(PROVERBS 8:13)

Central Focus: Pride and arrogance are a stench in the nostrils of the Almighty, and they must be avoided at all costs. They are destructive to every relationship in our lives—with God, other people, and even ourselves. Repentance and humility are the only solutions to pride and arrogance.

Prayer: O God, my Father, it grieves me to realize that I have had an arrogant attitude too often in my life, and I am asking you to help me replace it with true humility. I know that you resist the proud and give grace to the humble. Therefore, I ask you to clothe me with humility. As I repent of all arrogance and pride, I choose to humble myself under your mighty hand. Thank you for your promise to exalt me in due time when I do so.

I give reverence and honor to you, Lord, for I know that this brings wisdom and humility to me. Thank you for showing me that humility comes before honor. Riches, honor, and life come through humility and fearing you. Help me, Lord, to fear you and to serve you with all humility of mind. It will be my everlasting joy to do so.

Through your grace and power, I will walk worthy of the vocation to which you have called me, and I will do so with all lowliness, meekness, and longsuffering as I forbear with others in love. I will endeavor to keep the unity of the Spirit in the bond of peace.

Lord, it is my desire to fulfill your joy by being like-minded with you and all believers, having the same love, and being of one accord and one mind with you and them. Because of your strength, I will do nothing through strife or vainglory, but in lowliness of mind I will esteem others as better than myself. Help me, Father, to do so all the time.

May I never forget that pride produces shame and contention. It is so true that pride goes before destruction and that pride will bring me low. Therefore, I determine in my heart, Father, to love not the world and the things that are in the world, for I know that when I love the world, I do not experience your love. All that is in the world—the lust of the flesh, the lust of the eyes, and the pride of life—are not from you. They come from the world and the evil one and I want nothing to do with them.

It is my desire to do your will, Lord, and I thank you for your promise that I will abide forever. I praise you, Lord.

In Jesus' name I pray, Amen.

Scriptures: 1 Peter 5:5-6; Proverbs 15:33; Proverbs 22:4; Proverbs 20:19; Ephesians 4:1-3; Ephesians 2:2-3; Proverbs 11:2; Proverbs 13:10; Proverbs 16:18; Proverbs 29:23; 1 John 2:15-17.

Personal Affirmation: I confess that I have had an arrogant attitude at various times during my life. I fully repent of all pride and arrogance as I determine in my heart to clothe myself with humility. I will walk humbly before others as I humble myself under God's almighty hand. Arrogance is so destructive, but humility brings peace and joy. Hallelujah!

Reflection: *"Humility is the root, motive, nurse, foundation, and bond of all virtue"* (John Chrysostom).

3

Back to Basics

But seek first the kingdom of God, and His righteousness, and all these things shall be added to you.

(MATTHEW 6:33 NKJV)

Central Focus: Our relationship with God is the primary thing, and stemming from it are faith, prayer, Bible study, Christian fellowship, worship, and so many other basic things. We should not lose sight of these basics, for they are the true foundation of our faith.

Prayer: O God, I desire to go back to the basics of my Christian faith. I remember when I first realized how much you love me. Thank you for giving your only begotten Son, the Lord Jesus. Because of Him I know I will have everlasting life. Thank you, Lord, for this rich and wonderful promise.

The greatest moment of my life was when I received Jesus as my Savior, for it was then that you gave me your power to become your child as a result of receiving Him and believing on His name. From that point on my love for you and others grew, as did my love for your Word which is a lamp unto my feet and a light unto my path.

Your Word is quick and powerful, and it is sharper than any two-edged sword. It is able to pierce to the dividing asunder of the joints and marrow, and it is a discerner of the thoughts and intents of my heart. I love your Word, Father.

Help me to walk in the light, truth, and power of your Word each step of my way. Thank you for teaching me to study and pray your Word. By so doing I have discovered how to be a workman who is never ashamed because I know how to rightly teach your principles. I will hide your Word in my heart so as to never sin against you, and I will pray without ceasing.

Help me to worship you in spirit and in truth, for I know you seek such worshippers and I want to be one of them. Deliver me from evil, Father, and restore my soul. My heart's desire is to know you, Lord, in the power of your resurrection and the fellowship of your sufferings. This one thing I do: forgetting those things that are behind and reaching out to those things that are before, I press toward the mark for the prize of your high calling in Christ Jesus.

Lord, I ask you to abide in me, as I learn to abide in you. You are the vine, and I am just a branch in your vine. By abiding in you I know I will be a very fruitful vine. I will let your words abide in me, Lord, and I know you will give to me whatever I ask of you. It is a certain truth that without you I can do nothing. Through you, however, I can do all things.

Help me always to not be distracted and to keep the basics of my faith in my mind.

In the wonderful name of Jesus I pray, Amen.

Scriptures: John 3:16; John 1:12; Psalm 119:105; Hebrews 4:12; 1 Timothy 2:15; Psalm 119:11; 1 Thessalonians 5:17; John 4:23; Luke 11:4; Psalm 23:3; Philippians 3:10; Philippians 3:13-14; John 15:4-7; Philippians 4:13.

Personal Affirmation: Remembering the important things of the faith, the basic truths upon which I have built my life, I will cling to these elementals and seek the Lord first and always. As I do so, I know He will bless me and mine. I will stand upon the foundation that Jesus has laid for me. I will live according to the basic truths He has imparted to me.

Reflection: *"God never made a promise that was too good to be true"* (Dwight L. Moody).

4

Bashfulness

For God has not given us a spirit of fear, but of power and of love and of a sound mind

(2 TIMOTHY 1:17 NKJV)

Central Focus: Bashfulness stems from fear and a lack of confidence. God wants us to be bold through the power of His Spirit instead of being intimidated by others. He wants us to be ". . . strong in the Lord, and in the power of his might" (Ephesians 6:10).

Prayer: Lord God, I realize that bashfulness sometimes keeps me from serving you in the way I would like. I ask you to keep me from being shy and timid in front of others. Gird me with your strength, which will make my way perfect.

You are my light and my salvation. Whom shall I fear? You are the strength of my life. Of whom shall I be afraid? I will wait upon you, O Lord, and thereby I will be of good courage as you strengthen my heart. Hallelujah for all the promises of your Word.

In you, O Lord, do I place my trust. Let me never be

ashamed or bashful. Deliver me in your righteousness. Bow down your ear to me. Deliver me speedily. Be my strong rock, lead me and guide me I pray.

May I never forget that fearing others is a great snare in my life. I choose to put my trust in you, Lord, and I know you will keep me safe. Father, there is no fear in love, and I know your perfect love casts out all fear from me. I know that when I am fearful or bashful I have not been made perfect in love. Father, help me to experience your love and to walk in love at all times.

Thank you for the power of the Holy Spirit, who has come upon me. He it is that enables me to be an effective witness for Jesus Christ. In my heart, I know that it is not by might nor by power, but by your Spirit that I shall prevail over all bashfulness. Thank you, Father.

In the powerful name of my Redeemer I pray, Amen.

Scriptures: Psalm 18:32; Psalm 27:1-2; Psalm 27:14; Psalm 30:1-3; Proverbs 29:25; 1 John 4:18; Ephesians 5:2; Acts 1:8; Zechariah 4:6.

Personal Affirmation: I determine not to cast away the confidence and strength the Lord has given to me. Through His grace, I will not allow others to intimidate me. I know that He will see me through whatever He calls me to do. His power is at work within me, so I never have to be bashful again. He has shown me that I have no reason to ever be ashamed or bashful about anything.

Reflection: *"Those blessings are sweetest that are won with prayer and worn with thanks"* (Thomas Goodwin).

5

Carelessness

Therefore my beloved brethren, be steadfast, immovable, always abounding in the work of the Lord, knowing that you labor is not in vain in the Lord.

(1 CORINTHIANS 15:58 NKJV)

Central Focus: Carelessness has no place in the life of a believer in Jesus Christ, for carelessness is a sin that involves not paying attention, being neglectful of one's responsibilities, being inconsiderate of others, and not thinking before acting or speaking. Obedience is the antidote to carelessness.

Prayer: Abba-Father, help me to be a caring and responsible disciple who always wants to please you. I know I can never please you when I am careless. Therefore, I repent of all carelessness in my life, and I ask you to help me to walk in wisdom from this time forth.

Father, thank you for allowing me to abound in faith, utterance, knowledge, diligence, and love. Because

I so abound, I will no longer be careless about anything. It is my desire to give full diligence to your commandments and my responsibilities. I choose to not be lazy or slothful any longer. Through your grace, I will be a follower of those who through faith and patience inherit your promises.

Laying aside all carelessness, I receive your promises by which I am made a partaker of your divine nature. Thank you, Lord, for enabling me to escape the corruption that is in the world through lust. Giving all diligence, I add virtue to my faith, knowledge to my virtue, temperance to my knowledge, patience to my temperance, godliness to my patience, brotherly kindness to godliness, and charity to brotherly kindness. Because of these things, I shall neither be barren nor unfruitful in the knowledge of my Lord Jesus Christ.

No longer will I be careless. Instead, with your help I will be diligent. Thank you for your promise that the hand of the diligent makes one rich in every way. In your Word you promise that that the hand of the diligent shall bear rule. Thank you, Father, for equipping me to be a leader.

My thoughts will be toward diligence at all times, and I know this will lead to your blessing in every area of my life. Thank you, Lord. Help me to stay undefiled in the way and to always follow your laws. I want to be your obedient child and to keep your testimonies at all times. Keep me from iniquity and evil so that I will walk in all your ways. You have commanded me to keep your precepts diligently, and I will do this always. When I have respect unto all your commandments I will no longer be ashamed.

I know, Lord God, that it is impossible to please you without faith. I believe in you with all my heart and I know that you are a rewarder of all who diligently seek you. The faith you have imparted to me will keep me from all carelessness. Thank you, Lord.

In Jesus' holy name I pray, Amen.

Scriptures: 2 Corinthians 8:7; Hebrews 6:11-12; 2 Peter 1:4-8; Proverbs 10:4; Proverbs 12:24; Proverbs 21:5; Proverbs 21:5; Psalm 119:1-6; Hebrews 11:6.

Personal Affirmation: As I learn to focus on the Lord and His ways, I will avoid carelessness in my life. He will guide me and direct me to always be steadfast, immovable, diligent, and obedient. These are the qualities that will keep me from ever being lazy, irresponsible, or careless. Through God's Word I've learned that carelessness is my enemy and I will avoid it at all costs.

Reflection: *"Lord, when I feel that what I am doing is insignificant and unimportant, help me to remember that everything I do is significant and important in your eyes, because you love me and you put me here, and no one else can do what I am doing in exactly the way I do it"* (Brennan Manning).

6

Carnal-mindedness

For to be carnally minded is death; but to be spiritually minded is life and peace.

(ROMANS 8:6)

Central Focus: Carnal-mindedness is a mind-set that is based on the desires of the flesh. It disregards the spiritual side of life and leads to the lust of the eyes and the lust of the flesh. It results in spiritual death and is to be avoided at all times. It is far better to be spiritually minded, because this leads to life and peace.

Prayer: My dear Father, I come to you now to ask for your help in dealing with carnal-mindedness in my life. It has taken away my joy, peace, and even my ability to love. I need your help with this. It has also driven me away from you.

Help me always to remember that the carnal mind is enmity against you, for it is not and cannot be subject to your laws. Carnal-mindedness keeps me from pleasing you, and I do want to please you, Lord. I thank you for the law of the Spirit of Life in Christ Jesus, which has set me free from the law of sin and death. I want the same Spirit that raised Christ from the dead to dwell in me so that my body (and my spirit) would be quickened to walk in newness of life.

Father, I now realize that those who are after the flesh mind the things of the flesh, but they that are after the Spirit mind the things of the Spirit. Father, I want to be of the Spirit; I want your Holy Spirit to reign in my life. I want to produce the fruit of the Spirit in all that I do. I want to experience the daily adventure that comes from being after the Spirit.

As a Christian, I now know that my nature is dead because of sin, but the Spirit within me is life because of righteousness. I am a debtor not to the flesh, to live after the flesh. Being in debt to the flesh will lead to death, but I choose to mortify the deeds of my body through the power of your Holy Spirit. Thank you for showing me that those who are led by the Spirit of God are your children. So lead me, Lord, for I want to live always as your child.

How I thank you that I have received the spirit of adoption which enables me to cry, "Abba, Father." Abba, I am your adopted child! Hallelujah! And if I am your child, I am your heir—a joint-heir with Jesus Christ. I am willing to suffer with Him so that we may be glorified together, for I know that the sufferings of this present time are not worthy to be compared with the glory that will be revealed in me.

Thank you for the power of the Holy Spirit, which

helps me when I am weak. Thank you for His intercession for me. I know that all things work together for good in my life. I love you, Father. Thank you for calling me according to your purpose.

It thrills me to know that you foreknew me and predestinated me to be conformed to the image of your Son, Jesus Christ, that He might be the firstborn among many brethren. Thank you for calling me, justifying me, and glorifying me. I know you are for me; therefore, I know that nothing or no one can be victorious when they are against me.

It blesses me so much to know that nothing—tribulation, distress, persecution, famine, nakedness, peril, sword, nor any other thing--will ever be able to separate me from your love through Christ Jesus my Lord. Indeed, I am more than a conqueror through Him.

Thank you for every promise of your Word, Father. I love you with all my heart.

In Jesus' name I pray, Amen.

Scriptures: Romans 8:7-8; Romans 8:2; Romans 8:11; Romans 8:5; Galatians 6:22-23; Romans 8-10-18; Romans 8:26; Romans 8:28; Romans 8:29-31; Romans 8:35-39.

Personal Affirmation: It is vitally important for me to walk after the Spirit, not after the flesh, and I will do so from this point forward. I realize that it is only by doing so that I shall I be able to be a true conqueror. Walking after the Spirit will keep me from fulfilling the lusts of my flesh. I now choose to put all forms of carnal-mindedness behind me.

Reflection: *"God will answer your prayers better than you think. Of course, one will not always get exactly what he has asked for. ... We all have sorrow and disappointments, but one must never forget that, if commended to God, they will issue in good. ... His own solution is far better than any we could conceive"* (Fanny J. Crosby).

7

Deception

Take heed that you not be deceived

(LUKE 21:8 NKJV)

Central Focus: Many who are deceived do not even know that they are being led astray. In fact, this is the root of deception and the result of it is spiritual blindness. The great deceiver is Satan, and he is the father of lies. The truth is not in him. God's Word is truth, and as you learn to hide His Word in your heart, you will not be deceived. The truth will make you free. (See John 8:32.)

Prayer: Father, I thank you for your Word. Its truth sets me free from all deception. With your help, I will no longer be deceived in any area of my life. So many in our time are being deceived by the evil one, and as a result of this widespread deception they think that fornication, idolatry, adultery, effeminacy, abuse, and so many other evil practices are acceptable. Thank you for showing me that such people will not inherit your kingdom. I ask that you would reveal this to them as well.

It is so good to know that I have been washed, sanctified, and justified by your Holy Spirit in the name of the Lord Jesus. I realize now, Father, that all things are lawful unto me, but I know that many things are not expedient for me. I will not allow myself to be brought under the power of such things. Thank you for revealing to me that you will not be mocked and that whatsoever I sow is what I will reap. If I sow to the flesh, I will reap corruption, but if I sow to the Spirit, I will reap life everlasting. This is good news indeed!

Help me, Lord, to never speak evil of others, and to show meekness toward all. I confess that in the past I was sometimes foolish, disobedient, and deceived. I served various lusts and pleasures, lived in malice and envy, and was hateful. After your kindness and love appeared, however, I was set free from each of these deceptions. Thank you for your kindness and love toward me. I will be forever grateful to you.

I place all my trust in you, O Lord. Let me never be ashamed. Deliver me in your righteousness. Bow down your ear toward me, and deliver me speedily. Be my strong rock and my defense. Save me from all deception. You are my rock and my fortress. Therefore, for your name's sake I ask you to lead me and guide me.

Be pleased, O Lord, to deliver me from all deception and to make haste to help me. Deliver me from deceitful and unjust people. You are the God of my strength. Oh, send out your light and your truth. Let them lead me. Deliver me from my enemies, O God. Defend me from all who rise up against me. Deliver me from the workers of iniquity and save me from bloodthirsty people.

Through your grace I will stand fast in the liberty wherewith Christ has made me free, and I will no longer be entangled by any yoke of bondage. Thank you for removing the bondage of deception from me and for enabling me to enter into the glorious liberty of your children.

I am free indeed. Hallelujah!

In the name of Jesus I pray, Amen.

Scriptures: 1 Corinthians 5:9-10; 1 Corinthians 5:11-12; Galatians 6:7-8; Titus 3:1-4; Psalm 31:1-3; Psalm 40:13; Psalm 43:1-3; Psalm 59:1-2; Galatians 5:1; Romans 8:21.

Personal Affirmation: By taking heed to and walking in God's Word and His wisdom I will recognize any attempts from the enemy to deceive me. I will no longer be deceived. Instead, I will walk in victory and liberty throughout my life. The agony of deception is now completely behind me. Praise the Lord!

Reflection: *"If you want to become fully mature in the Lord, you must learn to love the truth. Otherwise, you will always leave open a door of deception for the enemy to take what is meant to be yours"* (Joyce Meyer).

8

Dejection

Why are you cast down, O my soul? And why are you disquieted within me? Hope in God; for I shall yet praise Him, the help of my countenance and my God.

(PSALM 42:5 NKJV)

Central Focus: The Bible is quite clear in showing us that God does not want us to be depressed, sad, or dejected in any way. He wants us to learn to rejoice and to know that His joy is our strength. (See Nehemiah 8:10.) Instead of living a dejected life, God wants us to place our hope and trust in Him. He wants us to praise Him. Through prayer, trusting God, and believing His promises God will lift you out of all despair and dejection. Praise His holy name!

Prayer: As the hart pants after the water brooks, so does my soul pant after you, O God. Indeed, my soul thirsts for you, the living God. My tears have been flowing freely both day and night. O my God, my soul has been cast down within me. This causes me to ask, "Why are you cast down, O my soul? Why are you disquieted within me?" Through your grace, Father, I will praise you, for I know you are the health of my countenance and my God.

Your joy is my strength, dear Lord, therefore I will rejoice evermore, pray without ceasing, and give thanks to you in everything, for I know this is your will in Christ Jesus concerning me.

You are my Shepherd; therefore, I shall not want. You make me lie down in green pastures, and you lead me beside the still waters. You restore my soul, and you lead me in the paths of righteousness for your name's sake. Yea, though I walk through the valley of the shadow of death, I will fear no evil, for I know you are with me. Your rod and your staff bring great comfort to me. Thank you for preparing a table before me in the midst of my enemies and for anointing my head with oil. My cup overflows. Surely goodness and mercy will follow me all the days of my life, and I will dwell in your house forever.

Knowing these things lifts me above all dejection and depression. Thank you, Father. I put my trust in you and I rejoice. I will always shout for joy because I know you always defend me. I love your name, and I will always be joyful in you. Thank you for blessing me with your favor, Father.

I have set you always before me. I thank you that you are at my right hand, and because this is so, I know I will never be moved. My heart is glad and my soul rejoices. My flesh rests in hope, for I know that you will not leave me alone. Thank you for showing me the path of life. In your presence there is fullness of joy and at your right hand there are pleasures forevermore. Father, I want to abide in your presence always.

My God, I bless you, for you have begotten me unto a lively hope by the Resurrection of Jesus Christ from the dead. Thank you for giving me an incorruptible and undefiled inheritance that will never fade away, for it is reserved in Heaven for me. Thank you for keeping me by your power through faith unto salvation.

No longer dejected, I greatly rejoice. I realize, Father, that the trial of my faith is more precious than gold that perishes though it be tried by fire, that it may be found unto praise and honor and glory at the appearing of Jesus Christ. Though I have never seen Him, I love Him and believe in Him. I rejoice with unspeakable joy that is full of glory as I receive the end of my faith, which is the salvation of my soul.

Lord, I thank you and praise you for delivering me completely from dejection.

In the joyful name of Jesus I pray, Amen.

Scriptures: Psalm 42; Nehemiah 8:10; 1 Thessalonians 5:16-18; Psalm 23; Psalm 5:11-12; Psalm 16:8-11; 1 Peter 1:3-9.

Personal Affirmation: Walking in joy and gladness, I have no reason to be dejected any longer. God has set me free, gloriously free, as I surrender my life to Him. Hallelujah! When I am tempted to be sad or depressed, I will hope and trust in Him, for He is my King and my omnipotent God. I will abide in His presence forever.

Reflection: *"Mental pain is less dramatic than physical pain, but it is more common and also more hard to bear. The frequent attempt to conceal mental pain increases the burden: it is easier to say 'My tooth is aching' than to say 'My heart is broken'"* (C.S. Lewis).

9

Edginess

Be anxious for nothing, but in everything by prayer and supplication, with thanksgiving, let your requests be made known to God. And the peace of God, which surpasses all understanding, will guard your hearts and minds through Christ Jesus.

(PHILIPPIANS 4:6-7 NKJV)

Central Focus: Edginess is a form of anxiety and irritability that keeps a person from peace and rest. This is never God's will for anyone. He offers us His rest and peace, which will overcome all edginess. The key to overcoming this challenge is to go deeper into the Word of God and to let His Word wash you and renew your mind. Jesus said, "Peace I leave with you, my peace I give unto you: not as the world giveth, give I unto you. Let not your heart be troubled, neither let it be afraid" (John 14:27).

Prayer: Father God, I come to you now in the name of Jesus to seek your help in overcoming all edginess, anxiety, and nervousness in my life. I know you are able to help me with this. Thank you, Lord.

Thank you for justifying me and giving me your peace through the Lord Jesus Christ. It is by Him that I have access by faith into your grace. I stand and walk in your grace, Lord, and I rejoice in the hope of your glory.

Thank you for your kingdom, Father, which does not consist of meat and drink, but of righteousness, peace, and joy in the Holy Spirit. In Him I find my rest and peace. Thank you for helping me to overcome all forms of edginess in my life.

O God of hope, fill me with all joy and peace in believing, that I may abound in hope through the power of the Holy Spirit. I realize that there can be no edginess in my life when the Holy Spirit fills me. Thank you, Father, the God of peace, for bruising Satan under my feet and for giving me your grace, which is always with me.

I thank you for calling me to peace, Father. You are not the author of confusion, but of peace. I thank you that Jesus is my peace; it is He who brings unity to the Body of Christ. I will let your peace rule in my heart, Lord, and I will let your Word dwell in me richly in all wisdom, as I teach and admonish others. Whatever I do in word or deed I shall do in the name of the Lord Jesus, giving thanks to you by Him.

Perfect peace comes to me when I trust you fully and keep my mind stayed on you, Lord. I will ever trust in you and do good. In this way, I know I shall dwell in the land and be fed. I will delight myself in you, Lord, and I know you will give me the desires of my heart. I will commit my way unto you, and I know you will bring it to pass. I rest in you, as I wait patiently for you. I cease from all anger, irritability, and edginess, and I forsake all anger and wrath in my life.

Thank you for setting me free from all edginess, Father. I will henceforth walk in your peace and rest.

In Jesus' name I pray, Amen.

Scriptures: Romans 5:1-2; Romans 14:17; Romans 15:33; 1 Corinthians 7:15; 1 Corinthians 14:33; Ephesians 2:14; Colossians 3:15-17; Isaiah 26:3; Psalm 37:3-8.

Personal Affirmation: God has brought peace to my soul and complete freedom from all edginess and irritability. I will stand fast in the freedom He has given to me and I will not ever allow myself to be entangled again by that yoke of bondage. What a joy it is to know His peace that surpasses all understanding.

Reflection: *"No man is greater than his prayer life. The pastor who is not praying is playing; the people who are not praying are straying. We have many organizers, but few agonizers; many players and payers, few prayers; many singers, few clingers; lots of pastors, few wrestlers; many fears, few tears; much fashion, little passion; many interferers, few intercessors; many writers, but few fighters. Failing here [in prayer], we fail everywhere"* (Leonard Ravenhill).

10

Freedom

And you shall know the truth, and the truth shall make you free

(JOHN 8:32 NKJV)

Central Focus: Through the Lord Jesus Christ we are free indeed. He died to set us free from sin, self, and Satan. We must, therefore, stand fast in the liberty wherewith Christ has made us free and not be entangled ever again with any yoke of bondage. (See Galatians 5:1.) It was for freedom that Christ has set us free.

Prayer: O my Father, I thank you for setting me free. Your Son, Jesus Christ, is the way, the truth, and the life, and it is through Him that I find true spiritual freedom—a freedom so wonderful that it is difficult to describe.

Having been set free from sin, I am now a servant of righteousness. I yield all of my life and every part of my body to serve righteousness unto holiness. Thank you, Father, for all the promises of your Word. I know that there is now no condemnation for me because I am in Christ Jesus, and I walk not after the flesh but after the Spirit, for the law of the Spirit of Life in Christ Jesus has set me free from the law of sin and death.

With your help, Lord God, I will stand fast in the liberty wherewith Christ has made me free, and I will never allow myself to ever be entangled with a yoke of bondage again. Thank you for calling me to liberty, Lord. I will never use my liberty for an occasion for my flesh, but by love I will serve others. Thank you for showing me that all the Law is fulfilled in this: to love you with every part of my being and to love others as myself.

As I walk in the Spirit, I know I will not fulfill the lusts of my flesh. With your help, Father, I will continue to look into the perfect law of liberty. I will not be a forgetful hearer. Instead, I will be a doer of your Word. Hallelujah!

Lord God, you have emancipated me from sin, Satan, and the lusts of my flesh. I am free from the fear of the future and free from the guilt of the past. Through your power and grace, I am totally free, praise the Lord, free at last!

In Jesus' name I pray, Amen.

Personal Affirmation: I will stand fast in the glorious liberty God has given to me through Christ. I will not turn back to the old ways, and I will continue to walk in the Spirit, knowing that as I do so, I will not fulfill the lusts of my flesh. The goodness of God has led me to repentance, and I will serve Him for the rest of my days. (See Romans 2:4.)

Scriptures: John 14:6; John 8:32; John 8:36; Romans 6:18-19; Romans 8:1-2; Galatians 5:1; Galatians 5:13-16; Galatians 5:16; James 1:25.

Reflection: *"It is the truth of grace and not of the Law that brings you true freedom. The truth of the Law only binds you. In fact, religious bondage is one of the most crippling bondages with which a person can be encumbered. Religious bondage keeps one in constant fear, guilt, and anxiety"* (Joseph Prince).

11

Guilt

*If we confess our sins, he is faithful and just
to forgive us our sins, and to cleanse us from
all unrighteousness.*

(1 JOHN 1:9)

Central Focus: It is important for us to distinguish between actual guilt and guilt feelings. The Bible gives us a strong antidote for guilt, and that is found through the confession of our sins. The blood of Jesus Christ, our Lord, cleanses us from all sin. (See 1 John 1:7.) God forgives all who confess their sins and repent of them, and this removes all guilt from us.

Prayer: O Lord my God, I want to thank you for setting me free from all guilt. All guilt from the past is now completely gone, and so is my fear of the future. I thank you for the blood of Jesus which has cleansed me from all sin—past, present, and future. Hallelujah!

One of the many promises in your Word declares to me that there is no longer any condemnation (guilt) in my life, because I am in Christ Jesus and I no longer walk after the flesh, but after the Spirit. The law of the Spirit of life in Christ Jesus has set me free from the law of sin and death.

I bless you, Lord, and all that is within me blesses your holy name. I will never forget all the benefits you've given to me. You have forgiven all my iniquities and you have healed all my diseases. You have redeemed my life from destruction and you have crowned me with lovingkindness and tender mercies. Thank you, Father.

You satisfy my mouth with good things, and you renew my youth like the eagle's. You have executed righteousness and judgment in my behalf. Thank you for always being merciful and gracious, slow to anger, and loving toward me.

I am truly happy, Father, for I know that you have forgiven all my iniquities and you have covered my sins. I know that you will no longer impute sin to me. Hallelujah! As your follower, I want to always be kind to others, tender-hearted, and forgiving, because you have forgiven me for Christ's sake. Help me to walk in love, as Christ has loved me. How I praise you that He gave Himself for me as an offering and a sacrifice to you.

I give thanks to you , Father, for qualifying me to be a partaker of the inheritance of the saints in the light and for delivering me from the power of darkness and translating me into the Kingdom of your dear Son. Through the blood of the Lord Jesus Christ I know I have redemption and the forgiveness of all my sins. I no longer have to experience guilt because of them.

Thank you for helping me to see that I have been quickened together with Christ through faith in you. Thank you for raising Him from the dead and for the wonderful hope this brings to me.

It is so wonderful to know that I no longer have to experience guilt in my life. Thank you for loving me so much.

In the loving name of Jesus I pray, Amen.

Scriptures: Romans 8:1-2; Psalm 103:1-8; Romans 4:7-8; Ephesians 4:31-5:1; Colossians 1:12-14; Colossians 2:13.

Personal Affirmation: Through the blood of Jesus Christ I am totally free from all guilt. I will stand fast in this freedom. (See Galatians 5:1.) Like fear, guilt brings great torment, and I've experienced so much of that in the past. It will no longer be a part of my life. Hallelujah! It has been replaced by the love of God and His great mercy.

Reflection: *"The beauty of life is, while we cannot undo what is done, we can see it, understand it, learn from it, and change so that every new moment is spent not in regret, guilt, fear, or anger, but in wisdom, understanding and love"* (Jennifer Edwards).

12

Hastiness

He who is slow to wrath has great under-standing. But he who is impulsive exacts folly.

(PROVERBS 14:29)

Central Focus: An old adages states (quite accurately): "Haste makes waste." God does not want us to be hasty, for hastiness involves being in a careless hurry. This is unwise. It is much better to proceed with caution, to wait upon the Lord, and to let His fruit of the Spirit (patience) have its perfect work in our lives, that we will be perfect and entire, wanting nothing. (See James 1:4.)

Prayer: Lord, I ask that you would keep me from being hasty about anything. Fill me afresh with the Holy Spirit, that I would produce His fruit in all the relationships and responsibilities of my life. Your fruit is love, joy, peace, longsuffering (patience), gentleness, goodness, faith, meekness, and temperance. Help me to walk in the Spirit each step of my way.

Lord, you are ever patient, merciful, and forgiving. I want to be like you. Help me to be patient at all times and never hasty. Help me to remember what your Word says, Father, that the end of a thing is better than the beginning of it, and to be patient in spirit is better than to be proud or hasty in spirit. I will not allow myself to be hasty in my spirit to be angry. Instead, I will always strive, with your help, to be patient.

As you lead me, Lord, I will show love without hypocrisy and abhor that which is evil. Instead, I will cling to that which is good and be kindly affectionate toward others with brotherly love. In honor I will prefer others over myself. I will not be slothful in business. Instead, I will be fervent in spirit, as I continue to serve you. Help me to rejoice in hope, to be patient in tribulations, and to continue in prayer.

Lord, help me to ever be mindful of my responsibilities to be hospitable and to give to the needy. I will bless those who persecute me and rejoice with those who rejoice. I will also weep with those who weep. Help me not to give my attention to high things and not to recompense evil for evil. I want to live in peace with all, so I ask that you would help me to not avenge myself or allow myself to become full of wrath. Through your grace, Father, I will not be overcome by evil, but I will overcome evil with good.

It is my heart's desire to be patient until the coming of the Lord. Therefore, I will establish my heart, for I know that the Lord's coming draws near and I look forward to His coming.

Father, help me to glory in tribulations, because I know that tribulation works patience and longsuffering into me. Patience, then, works experience, and experience gives me hope. Thank you for showing me that hope will keep me from ever being ashamed, because your love is shed abroad in my heart by the Holy Spirit you've given to me.

Keep me from ever being hasty, Lord, for I know that it is through patience that I will be able to inherit your promises. Help me to walk worthy of you, fully pleasing, being fruitful in every good work and increasing in the knowledge of you. Through your grace I will be strengthened with all might, according to your glorious power, unto all patience and longsuffering with joyfulness. I will always give thanks unto you, Father, for you have made me able to be a partaker of the saints in light.

With great care, therefore, I will always endeavor to follow you. I will no longer be hasty in spirit, but patient even in times of persecution and tribulation. Thank you, Father.

In Jesus' loving name I pray, Amen.

Scriptures: Galatians 5:22-25; Numbers 14:18; Ecclesiastes 7:8-9; Romans 12:9-21; James 5:7-8; Romans 5:3-5; Hebrew 6:12; Colossians 1:10-12.

Personal Affirmation: I confess that I have acted hastily in times past. From this time forward I will endeavor to be patient with others and with all circumstances. I will proceed with caution and great care as I go forward to be like Jesus Christ, my Savior and Lord. I want to be like Him at all times. I will bear the fruit of patience in all the responsibilities and relationships of my life.

Reflection: *"Today, Lord, I am going to do my best with your help and for your glory. I realize that there are many different people in the world with a variety of opinions and expectations. I will concentrate on being a God-pleaser and not a self-pleaser or a man-pleaser. The rest I leave in your hands, Lord. Grant me favor with you and with men and continue transforming me into the image of your dear Son. Thank you, Lord"* (Joyce Meyer).

13

Heartache

*Fear not, nor be dismayed, be strong and of
good courage.*

(JOSHUA 10:25)

Central Focus: Heartache can be caused by a variety
of circumstances and challenges, such as the loss
of a loved one, a job, a pet, or a relationship. It might
also be caused by health issues. These would all
fall under the label of circumstantial depression.
Whatever the case, the Bible provides us with many
blessings to deal with heartache, and these include
faith, hope, joy, and trust. As we learn to trust in the
Lord with all our hearts, we experience His presence
and His guidance to help us deal with heartache.

Prayer: Father, thank you for blessing me with
every spiritual blessing in Christ Jesus. I will always
love you, O Lord, my strength. You are my rock, my
fortress, and my deliverer. You are my God and my
strength, and I will always trust in you. You are my
buckler, the horn of my salvation, and my high tower.

I will call upon you in my distress, and I know you will hear my voice. Thank you, Father, for lifting me out of the pit I have been in and for healing my broken-heartedness.

I wait patiently for you, O Lord. Thank you for inclining your ear toward me and hearing my cry. I know you are bringing me out of the pit of discouragement and you have set my feet upon a rock and have established all my goings. Thank you for putting a new song in my mouth, even the song of praise unto you. You are my trust, Father, and I know you will lead me into happiness.

Thank you for sending Jesus to bind up my broken heart and to proclaim liberty unto me. His comfort is restoring hope to me. Thank you for restoring my soul. I praise you for being the Father of mercies and the God of all comfort. I receive your comfort now in my time of tribulation. Because of you I can say that I am filled with comfort and I am joyful in this time of tribulation.

Your Word has quickened me and brought me comfort in my affliction. Thank you for your Word, Father, and all its rich and precious promises. It is through your Word that I receive patience, comfort, and hope.

Thank you for calling me through the gospel and allowing me to obtain the glory of our Lord Jesus Christ. I ask, Lord God, that you would enable me to stand fast and to hold to the traditions of the faith. I am so blessed to know how much you love me.

Thank you for giving me everlasting consolation and good hope through grace. Comfort my heart, and establish me in every good work.

In Jesus' blessed name I pray, Amen.

Scriptures: Ephesians 1:3; Psalm 18:1-6; Psalm 40:1-4; Isaiah 61:1-2; Psalm 23:3; 2 Corinthians 1:3-4; 2 Corinthians 7:4; Psalm 119:50; Romans 15:4; 2 Thessalonians 2:15-17.

Personal Affirmation: Through the power of God's grace I will take my stand against depression and discouragement. I will count it all joy when I fall into diverse temptations. (See James 1:2.) I reach out and take hold of God's mighty hand, and I know He is lifting me out of despair and heartache. He is my hope, my confidence, my strength, and my comfort. He is healing my heartache.

Reflection: *"Even the saddest things can become, once we have made peace with them, a source of wisdom and strength"* (Frederick Buechner).

14

Immaturity

*But speaking the truth in love, may grow up
into him in all things, which is the head, even
Christ.*

(EPHESIANS 4:15)

Central Focus: There is physical, psychological, and spiritual immaturity. All three come from a lack of motivation and growth. To be spiritually mature we must follow Jesus. We must be His disciple and obey Him in all things. It is essential to spiritual growth for us to walk in the Spirit, so we will not fulfill the lusts of our flesh. (See 2 Peter 2:10.) We must study God's Word daily. (See 2 Timothy 2:15.) We must pray without ceasing. (See 1 Thessalonians 5:17.) In this way, we will grow in the Lord and experience spiritual maturity, and spiritual maturity leads to maturity in all areas of life.

Prayer: O God, my heavenly Father, I need you to help me grow in grace and in the knowledge of my Lord Jesus Christ. Thank you for imparting your righteousness to me, which enables me to flourish like the palm tree and to grow like a cedar in Lebanon. I have been planted in your house, O Lord, and I know I shall flourish in your courts. It is wonderful to know that I shall bring forth fruit in old age.

My goal is in alignment with yours, Lord God. With other believers, I will come in the unity of the faith and of the knowledge of the Son of God, unto a perfect man, unto the measure of the stature of the fullness of Christ, that I would be no longer immature, tossed to and fro and carried about by every wind of doctrine, the sleight of men, and cunning craftiness. Instead, I will speak the truth in love and grow up into Christ in all things, for He is the Head of the Body.

Therefore, laying aside all malice, guile, hypocrisy, envy, and evil speaking, as a newborn baby, I desire the sincere milk of the Word that I may grow thereby. God, my Father, I have put on the new man, which is renewed in knowledge after your image. As one of your elect I put on tender mercies, kindness, humility, meekness, and longsuffering. I will forbear with others and forgive them, as well. Above all else, I will put on love, which is the bond of perfection. In so doing I will let your peace, which surpasses all understanding, rule in my heart and I will let your Word dwell in me richly in all wisdom. Whatever I do in word or in deed I will do in the name of my Lord Jesus Christ and I will give thanks unto you, O Father. In this way, I will know and practice spiritual maturity.

Father, I ask that you would grant me, according to the riches of Christ's glory to be strengthened with might by your Spirit within my inner being, that Christ may dwell in my heart by faith and that, being rooted and grounded in love, I will be able to comprehend with all saints what is the breadth, length, depth, and height, and that I would know the love of Christ, which surpasses knowledge and would be filled with all the fullness of God.

It is my desire to be wise, Father. Therefore, I will listen for your voice and increase in learning. Help me to listen to wise counsel. I will fear you, O Lord, and I know this will give me the spiritual knowledge I need. I will study to show myself approved unto you, Father, and by this I will become a workman who will never need to be ashamed because I know how to rightly divide your Word.

Thank you for working in me both to will and to do of your good pleasure. As I grow in you, I know I will learn to do all things without murmuring and disputing. Help me to be blameless and harmless as your child, without rebuke, in the midst of this crooked and perverse society. I will hold forth the word of life so that I may rejoice in the day of Christ. At that time I will know that I have not run nor labored in vain.

Thank you for helping me to attain to spiritual maturity, Father.

In Jesus' name I pray, Amen.

Scriptures: 2 Peter 3:18; Psalm 92:12-14; Ephesians 4:13-15; 1 Peter 2:1-2; Colossians 3:10-17; Ephesians 3:16-19; Proverbs 1:5; Proverbs 1:7; 2 Timothy 2:15;

Philippians 2:15-16.

Personal Affirmation: My greatest desire is to grow in the Lord. As I study His Word and spend time with Him, I know He will lead me, guide me, strengthen me, and help me in every way. I will seek first His will and His righteousness (see Matthew 6:33) and I know that He will add all things unto me. God is so good to me, and I will follow Him each step of my way.

Reflection: *"You are either becoming more like Christ every day or you are becoming less like Him. There is no neutral position in the Lord"* (Stormie Omartian).

15

Impulsiveness

He who is slow to anger is better than the mighty, and he who rules his spirit than he who takes a city.

(PROVERBS 16:32 NKJV)

Central Focus: When one is impulsive he is without control in certain areas of his life and will often act suddenly without considering the consequences of his actions. Such impulsiveness can lead to major difficulties in a person's life. That's why the Bible encourages us to rule (or control) our own spirits. Let us always remember that self-control is a fruit of the Holy Spirit in our lives.

Prayer: Heavenly Father, I love your Word. It tells me that if I want to strive for the mastery, I must be temperate in all things. Help me to practice moderation, temperance, and self-control at all times. I no longer want to be impulsive as I have been in times past.

Teach me how to walk in the Spirit, that I might not fulfill the lusts of my flesh. Impulsiveness is a work of my flesh, and I put it behind me now. Fill me with your Spirit, Father, that I would produce His fruit in all the relationships and responsibilities of my life—love, joy, peace, longsuffering, gentleness, goodness, faith, meekness, and temperance (self-control). Against such there is no law.

Thank you for all the promises of your Word, Lord. I will believe them, receive them, and appropriate them into my life so as to never be impulsive again. Your great and precious promises enable me to be a partaker of your divine nature, having escaped the corruption that is in the world through faith. Therefore, giving all diligence, I will add virtue to my faith, knowledge to my virtue, temperance to my knowledge, patience to my temperance, godliness to my patience, brotherly kindness to my godliness, and charity (love) to my brotherly kindness.

Thank you for showing me that if these things abound within me, they will keep me from being impulsive, barren, and unfruitful in my life and in the knowledge of the Lord Jesus Christ. Father, I ask sincerely that you would help me to be blameless, not self-willed, not easily angered, not violent, not greedy, but a lover of hospitality. Help me to be sober, just, holy and temperate as I hold fast your faithful Word as you have taught me.

Lord, instead of being impulsive and impatient, I will wait patiently on you. Thank you for hearing and answering my prayer. You have brought me out of a horrible pit that was filled with miry clay, and you have set my feet upon a rock and established me. Thank you for putting a new song in my heart, even a song of praise unto you. I have made you my trust, dear Lord. Hallelujah!

I will bless you at all times, Lord, and your praise shall continually be in my mouth. My soul will make its boast in you. The humble shall hear me and be glad. I will magnify you, Lord God, and I will exalt your name forever. I sought you, Lord, and you delivered me from my fears and my impulsiveness. I will always be thankful unto you.

In Jesus' precious name I pray, Amen.

Scriptures: 1 Corinthians 9:23; Galatians 5: 22-23; 2 Peter 1:4-9; Titus 1:7-9; Psalm 40:1-4; Psalm 34:1-4.

Personal Affirmation: Being impulsive has caused great problems in my life. I now repent of my impulsiveness and ask God to keep me in the center of His will. I put behind me all anger, restlessness, indecisiveness, and violence, and replace these negative attributes with kindness, tender-heartedness, and forgiveness. I thank God that He is enabling me to be a new person.

Reflection: *"Before you make a decision, ask yourself this question: will you regret the results or rejoice in them?"* (Rob Liano).

16

Inconsistency

Therefore, my beloved brethren, be stead-fast, immovable, always abounding in the work of the Lord, knowing that your labor is not in vain in the Lord.

(1 CORINTHIANS 15:58 NKJV)

Central Focus: A person who is inconsistent is not dependable because one never knows what to expect from them. A faithful person, on the other hand, can always be counted on to do his or her part. An inconsistent person is one who is changeable. He or she does not hold to the principles and practices that others expect of them. The inconsistent person needs to surrender his or her life to the Lord completely so that he or she will be steadfast, immoveable, and always abounding in the work of the Lord.

Prayer: Father, I thank you for your great faithfulness towards me. I want to be like you so I ask you to fill me afresh with the Holy Spirit so that I would become faithful like you and would never be inconsistent again. I need your help and strength to enable me to rise above all inconsistencies in my life.

I love you, Lord. Thank you for preserving me and plentifully rewarding me in so many ways. Therefore, I will be of good courage, for I know you will strengthen my heart. Hallelujah! You are my light and my salvation. You are the strength of my life. As I look to you, all inconsistency in my heart and life fade away.

An inconsistent person is often double-minded. Help me, Father, to never be double-minded again, for a double-minded person is unstable in all his ways. I want to have a single mind, heart, and soul that are totally devoted to you.

Teach me your way, O Lord, and lead me in a plain path. I will wait on you and be of good courage because I know you will strengthen me and help me to be more consistent. Help me always to be a faithful ambassador who brings life to all I come in contact with. Your Word promises me that a faithful person will abound with blessings. This is wonderful to know, and it causes me to want to be faithful and consistent at all times.

Father, forgive me for my inconsistency. I want always to please you. Therefore, I trust you and determine to do good consistently throughout my life. I will delight myself in you, and I know you will give me the desires of my heart. Thank you, Father. I commit my way unto you and completely trust in you, and I know you will answer my prayer to become more consistent before you and others.

I will trust in you with all my heart, without leaning unto my own understanding. In all my ways I will acknowledge you, and I know you will direct my paths. Thank you, Lord. As I learn to acknowledge you at all times, I know that inconsistency in my life will be a thing of the past.

Father, thank you so much for making my heart fixed, as I trust in you. You have established my heart, and I shall not be afraid or inconsistent any longer. I feel totally renewed in your presence.

Praise you, mighty God.

In Jesus' holy name I pray, Amen.

Scriptures: Lamentations 3:23; Psalm 31:23-24; Psalm 27:1; James1:8; Psalm 27:11-14; Proverbs 13:17; Proverbs 28:20; Psalm 37:3-7; Proverbs 3:5-6; Psalm 112:7-8.

Personal Affirmation: Consistency will come as I draw closer to the Lord and study His Word. I will walk in the wisdom and comfort of His Word each day. I know that the blood of Jesus Christ has cleansed me from all inconsistency. From this point forward I will be faithful, trustworthy, and steady. People will see that I am consistent in following the Lord and obeying Him.

Reflection: *"Do not have your concert first, and then tune your instrument afterwards. Begin the day with the Word of God and prayer, and get first of all into harmony with Him"* (James Hudson Taylor).

17

Inferiority Complex

I will praise You, for I am fearfully and wonderfully made.

(PSALM 139:14 NKJV)

Central Focus: God loves you, and He created you in His own image. These two facts, which are central to our faith, should keep every believer from ever feeling inferior. God has accepted us in His beloved (see Ephesians 1:6), and He has invited us into His banqueting hall. (See Song of Solomon 2:4.) His banner over us is love. For all these reasons, we must never feel inferior.

Prayer: Father, because I know you are for me, I know that nothing can be against me. There is, therefore, no condemnation in my life. I am in Christ Jesus, and I walk after His Spirit, not after the Law. How I praise you, Lord, that the law of the Spirit of life in Christ Jesus has set me free from the law of sin and death.

Thank you, Abba-Father, for adopting me into your family and for making me a joint-heir with Jesus. I praise you, Lord, for you have blessed me with all spiritual blessings in heavenly places in Christ. Hallelujah! Help me to remember that this has already happened. It is an accomplished fact.

Thank you for choosing me before the foundation of the world, that I would be holy and blameless before you in love. It thrills me to know that you have chosen me. Father, I thank you for giving me such a blessed inheritance. You have predestined me according to the purpose of Christ who works all things after the counsel of His own will.

Father of glory, I ask that you would give me the spirit of wisdom and revelation through my knowledge of Christ. Open the eyes of my understanding and enlighten me so that I would know what the hope of your calling is and I would know what the riches of the glory of your inheritance in the saints are. Thank you for revealing unto me the exceeding greatness of your power through faith.

Grant to me, according to the riches of your glory, to be strengthened with all might by your Spirit deep within me. I invite Christ to dwell in my heart by faith, that I, being rooted and grounded in love, may be able to comprehend with all the saints the breadth, length, depth, and height of your marvelous love. Father, I want to walk in the love of Christ, which surpasses knowledge so that I would be filled with all the fullness of God.

I praise your holy name, Lord, for I know that you are able to do exceeding abundantly above all that I ask or think, according to the power that works within me. Unto you be glory in the Church by Christ Jesus throughout all ages, world without end.

Thank you for freeing me from all feelings of inferiority by which I was so long deceived.

In the glorious name of Jesus I pray, Amen.

Scriptures: Romans 8:31; Romans 8:1-2; Romans 8:15-17; Ephesians 1:3-4; Ephesians 1:11; Ephesians 1:17-19; Ephesians 3:16-21.

Personal Affirmation: There is no reason whatsoever for me to ever feel inferior to others because I am God's child, and I was created in His image. Therefore, I will rise above the inferiority complex I was experiencing and I will be totally confident in the Lord. His power and strength embolden me. I have boldness and access with confidence by faith in Jesus, so I must never feel condemned, ashamed, or inferior again. (See Ephesians 3:11-12.)

Reflection: *"Your desire is your prayer. Picture the fulfillment of your desire now and feel its reality, and you will experience the joy of answered prayer"* (Joseph Murphy).

18

Intimacy with God

Draw near to God and He will draw near to you.

(JAMES 4:8 NKJV)

Central Focus: We were created to know God and to enjoy Him forever. He wants to have fellowship with us. To be intimate with God, we must learn to listen for His voice when we pray, give Him glory throughout each day, and seek His face. In His presence, there is fullness of joy and there are pleasures forevermore. (See Psalm 16:11.)

Prayer: Abba-Father, I love you with all my heart, mind, soul, and strength. Keep me as the apple of your eye, and hide me under the shadow of your wings. I will always love you, O Lord, my strength, for you are my rock, my fortress, and my deliverer. You are my God, my strength, and I will always trust in you.

In quietness and in confidence I find strength. Thank you, Father. I will learn to be still and know you as my God. I count all things as loss for the excellency of the knowledge of Christ Jesus my Lord. For Him I have suffered the loss of all things and do count them as dung so that I may win Christ and be found in Him, not having my own righteousness, which is of the Law, but that which is through the faith of Christ, the righteousness which comes through you, Father. My desire is to know Him and the power of His resurrection and the fellowship of His sufferings.

Thank you for wanting to have fellowship with me, Lord. Truly my fellowship is with you, Father, and with your Son, Jesus Christ. Thank you for your faithfulness to me, Father, and thank you for calling me into the fellowship of your Son, the Lord Jesus Christ.

Teach me to discern your voice when you speak to me. I am your sheep, and I will follow you each step of the way. The promises of your Word assure me that my intimacy with you will grow. Your Word is a lamp unto my feet and a light unto my path. I will walk in the light of your Word always, and I know you will never leave me nor forsake me. Hallelujah!

Thank you for reconciling me unto yourself and helping me to continue in the faith, grounded and settled. I will not allow myself to be moved away from the hope of the gospel, for it is my very life. The Holy Spirit bears witness with my spirit that I am your child.

Your everlasting love keeps me going, Father. Through your grace I will always endeavor to be faithful to you, as you are to me. I am so glad that you have searched me and known me. It is wonderful to know that you know when I sit down and when I rise up. It is an amazing truth that you discern my thoughts from afar.

Thank you for your wonderful promise, that as I draw near to you, you are drawing near to me.

In Jesus' holy name I pray, Amen.

Scriptures: Mark 12:30; Psalm 17:8; Psalm 18:1-2; Isaiah 30:15; Psalm 46:10; Philippians 3:8-10; 1 John 1:3; 1 Corinthians 1:9; John 10:27; Psalm 119:105; 2 Corinthians 5:19; Colossians 1:23; Romans 8:16; Psalm 139:1-25.

Personal Affirmation: The Lord is my everlasting and loving companion. I will walk with Him each step of the way. I want to know Him and to have fellowship with Him, so I will spend time in prayer, His Word, and His presence each day. I will speak to Him, and I will listen for His voice. This is my life's goal—to know my Lord in all His fullness and to share Him with others.

Reflection: *"I think the reason we sometimes have the false sense that God is so far away is because that is where we have put Him. We have kept Him at a distance, and then when we are in need and call on Him in prayer, we wonder where He is. He is exactly where we left Him."* (Ravi Zacharias).

19

Jealousy

Jealousy is cruel as the grave.

(SONG OF SOLOMON 8:6)

Central Focus: To be jealous is to be resentfully envious of others. It may even involve suspicion. Jealousy is to be avoided, for it is not only sin, but it is a form of deception from the evil one who seeks to destroy us in any way possible. It involves feelings of ill-will toward others when they do well or have things we desire. Instead of being jealous, we should rejoice with those who rejoice and bless them sincerely. (See Romans 12:15.)

Prayer: O God, my heavenly Father, I ask that you would forgive me for feelings of jealousy that I have held toward others. Thank you for showing me in your Word that a sound heart is the life of the flesh, and envy is the rottenness of the bones. I want to have a sound heart always.

It is envy that leads to jealousy, so I ask for your help to never let my heart envy sinners or anyone else.

Instead, I want to stay in a reverent attitude toward you, for I know this will keep me from all jealousy and envy. Help me to remember that godliness with contentment is great gain for me. If I am truly content, I know I will not entertain thoughts of jealousy or envy.

Father, I desire to be ready for every good work. Therefore, I will speak evil of no one. Through your grace I will be gentle and will show meekness toward all others. How I thank you for your kindness and love. Thank you for justifying me by your grace and making me an heir according to the hope of eternal life.

Keep me from all carnal-mindedness, Father, for I know that carnal-mindedness leads to death. Help me ever to walk honestly, as in the day, not in rioting, drunkenness, chambering, wantonness, strife, and envying. Instead of those things, I will put on the Lord Jesus Christ. By so doing I will not make any provision for my flesh to fulfill its lusts.

Jealousy and envy are works of the flesh. I ask you, Father, to help me avoid these by filling me afresh with the Holy Spirit so that I would be able to produce His fruit in all the relationships and responsibilities of my life—love, joy, peace, longsuffering, gentleness, goodness, faith, meekness, and temperance. Against these qualities there is no law.

When I used to have bitter envy, jealousy, and strife in my heart, I experienced great stress and confusion because those traits are not from above. They are earthly, sensual, and devilish. Your wisdom, Father, however, is pure, peaceable, gentle, easy to be entreated, full of mercy and good fruits. It is without partiality and hypocrisy. Thank you for the fruit of righteousness that is sown in peace by those who make peace.

I rejoice greatly in you, O Lord. Thank you for helping me to learn that in whatsoever state I am, therewith to be content. I can do all things through Christ who strengthens me. He is enabling me to overcome all jealousy.

In His mighty name I pray, Amen.

Scriptures: Proverbs 14:30; Proverbs 23:17; 1 Timothy 6:6; Titus 3:1-7; Romans 8:6; Romans 13:13-14; Galatians 5:19-26; James 3:15-18; Philippians 4:11-13.

Personal Affirmation: I put all envy and jealousy behind me now. Through Christ my Lord I will be content and at peace at all times. I will not allow myself to want what others have or do. I will be thankful for everything God has given to me instead of always desiring to have more. "I press toward the mark for the prize of the high calling of God in Christ Jesus" (Philippians 3:14).

Reflection: *"The cure for the sin of envy and jealousy is to find our contentment in God"* (Jerry Bridges).

20

Judgmentalism

Judge not, that you be not judged

(MATTHEW 7:1 NKJV)

Central Focus: We are not called to judge others. Judging others is one of the most negative things we can ever do. We should love others and leave the judging to God. Our focus should be on overcoming evil with good. (See Romans 12:21.)

Prayer: O God, help me not to be judgmental toward others. The way of every person is frequently right in his own eyes, but you, Father, ponder the hearts of people. I believe your Word which tells me that it is never good to judge others.

Instead of judging others, I want to help them. When I see others, who are overtaken in a fault or a sin, help me to restore them in a spirit of meekness. At such times I will consider myself, lest I also be tempted in the same realm. Help me to bear the burdens of others and so fulfill the law of Christ.

Help me to be forgiving toward others, Father. Through

your grace, I will bear with others and forgive them even as Christ has forgiven me. Strengthen me so that I will be able to put all bitterness, wrath, anger, clamor, and evil speaking away from me. I will replace those negative attributes with kindness, tender-heartedness, and forgiveness.

Thank you, Lord, for demonstrating your love toward me in that while I was yet a sinner Jesus died for me. Your love is an everlasting love, and I want to demonstrate your love toward others at all times. I realize, Lord, that I am able to love because you first loved me.

Therefore, instead of judging others, I will love them, for I know that love is of you and everyone who loves is born of you and knows you. Those who do not love, however, do not know you, for you are love. Faith, hope, and love abide, but the greatest of these is love.

Help me to abide in your love, Lord, and to keep my focus on ministering to and praying for others. I will remember that love never fails. Give me the strength and courage, Father, to love others as you have loved me and to remember that greater love has no one than this: to lay down one's life for a friend. I will obey your supreme commandment to love others.

I want always to obey your commandment to love others, as you have loved me, for through this others will know that I am your disciple. Though no one has seen you at any time, people are able to see you in me when I love others, and this is my greatest desire.

You abide in me, and your love has been perfected in me.

Because of all these marvelous truths, I know it is my responsibility to love others and not to judge them. Preserve me from any temptation toward judgmentalism.

In Jesus' name I pray, Amen.

Scriptures: Proverbs 21:2; Proverbs 24:23; Galatians 6:1-2; Colossians 3:13; Ephesians 4:31-32; Romans 5:8; Jeremiah 33:3; 1 John 4:19; 1 John 4:7-12; 1 Corinthians 13:13; John 15:9; 1 Corinthians 13:8; John 15:12-14, 17; John 13:34-35; 1 John 4:10-12.

Personal Affirmation: It is through the love of God that I am able to overcome all judgmentalism in my life. Therefore, I will follow after love and desire spiritual gifts. (See 1 Corinthians 14:1.) I will bear the burdens of others and thereby fulfill God's law. (See Galatians 6:2.) I am so thankful that God has delivered me from all judgmentalism.

Reflection: *"He that well and rightly considereth his own works will find little cause to judge hardly of another"* (Thomas a Kempis).

21

Loneliness

The eternal God is your refuge, and underneath are the everlasting arms.

(DEUTERONOMY 33:27 NKJV)

Central Focus: God is always with me, and He will never leave me nor forsake me. (See Hebrews 13:5.) There is no need for me to ever feel lonely, even when others forsake me, for He is my friend and He will be with me always. Draw close to God, and He will draw close to you. (See James 4:8.)

Prayer: Father God, I love and adore you. Therefore, I will let my conduct be without covetousness, and I will be content with such things as I have. I will always rejoice to know that you will never leave me nor forsake me. Hallelujah.

When I feel lonely, I will draw close to you. I will read your Word and meditate upon its truths. I will pray to you and listen for your voice. In so doing, I know I will sense your presence in which I will find fullness of joy and pleasures forevermore. Thank you for showing me the path of life.

Help me to teach your truths to others, Lord, so that they will observe all the things you have commanded. I rejoice to know your promise, "I am with you always, even to the end of the age." Thank you, also, for your promise to never forsake your people.

Even as I am praying, all loneliness is departing from me. I will not fear nor be dismayed because you are my God. Thank you for strengthening me and helping me. Thank you for upholding me with your righteous right hand.

It is thrilling to know that nothing shall ever be able to separate me from your love, Father. Thank you for your promise to heal the broken-hearted and to bind up all my wounds. Through the Holy Spirit I will not let my heart be troubled, because I believe in you and I believe in Jesus Christ my Lord. Thank you for the peace you've given to me in place of the loneliness I had before.

You are enabling me to be strong and of good courage, Father. Therefore, I will not fear, for I know you always go with me and you will not forsake me. I cast all my cares upon you, because I know you care for me. You are my refuge and my strength, and you will always be a very present help to me in times of trouble. Thank you, Lord.

Your promise still stands: "For the mountains shall depart, and the hills be removed; but my kindness shall not depart from thee, neither shall the covenant of my peace be removed, saith the Lord that hath mercy on thee."

No longer lonely, I now rejoice in your presence, Father. Thank you for always being with me.

Scriptures: James 4:8; Psalm 16:11; Matthew 18:20; 1 Samuel 12:22; Isaiah 41:10; Romans 8:39; Psalm 147:3; John 14:1; John 14:27; Deuteronomy 31:6; 1 Peter 1:7; Isaiah 54:10.

Personal Affirmation: I have no reason to be lonely, because God is always with me. When I feel lonely, I will seek Him through His Word, worship, prayer, and Christian fellowship. I know He will always be waiting for me. I will spend my time praising God and enjoying His presence. He is so good to me, and He has delivered me from all loneliness through His power and love.

Reflection: *"Answered prayer is the interchange of love between the Father and His child"*
(Andrew Murray).

22

Maintaining Hope

Now may the God of hope fill you with all joy and peace in believing, that you may abound in hope by the power of the Holy Spirit.

(ROMANS 15:13 NKJV)

Central Focus: Hope is the anchor of our souls. It helps us to stay focused on the things of God and His will for us. Hope, faith, and trust are intertwined, and each one enables us to stay on course. The opposite of hope is hopelessness, which leads to despair. Hope, on the other hand, enables us to believe that what is wanted will happen. It is a strong desire that is accompanied by expectation.

Prayer: Thank you, Father, for imparting your hope to me. Your hope keeps me from all shame. I thank you for your hope and your love, which is shed abroad in my heart by the Holy Spirit which you've given to me. You are my portion; therefore, I will always hope in you.

I ask that you would fill me with all joy and peace in believing, that I may abound in hope through the power of the Holy Spirit. I hope in your Word, Father. It is a lamp unto my feet and a light unto my path. O God, you are my hope, and I bless you. Thank you for always giving me counsel from your Word. I have set you always before me. Because you are at my right hand, I know I shall never be moved. Therefore, my heart is glad and my soul rejoices. My flesh shall always rest in the hope you've given to me. You have shown me the path of life. In your presence there is fullness of joy, and at your right hand there are pleasures forevermore.

In you, O Lord, do I hope. I know you will hear my prayer. O Lord my God. You are both my hope and my trust. Let my mouth be filled with your praise all day long. Remove any sense of hopelessness from me, Abba-Father, for I place all my hope in you. I will always hope in you, and I will always praise you for your constant help in my life. You are the health of my countenance, and I will ever praise you.

Help me to maintain the full assurance of hope until the end. Thank you, God of all hope, for filling me with joy and peace in believing, that I will be able to abound in hope through the power of the Holy Spirit.

In the name of Jesus I pray, Amen.

Scriptures: Romans 5:5; Lamentations 3:24; Romans 15:13; Psalm 119:114; Psalm 119:105; Psalm 16:5-11; Psalm 38:15; Psalm 71:5-8; Hebrews

6:11; Romans 15:13.

Personal Affirmation: God has filled me with hope. All hopelessness is gone from my life. I have placed all my hope and trust in the Lord. I know I can depend on Him.

Reflection: *"God is the only one who can make the valley of trouble a door of hope"* (Catherine Marshall).

23

Mental Confusion

For God is not the author of confusion, but of peace.

(1 CORINTHIANS 14:33)

Central Focus: Mental confusion never comes from God. Rather, it comes to us when we are not focused on the purpose to which we have been called. Knowing God and enjoying Him forever will keep us from mental confusion. He will lead us to live well-balanced and highly focused lives.

Prayer: Father God, I thank you for helping me to see and think clearly. Thank you for being the author of peace in my life. Help me never to be anxious about anything, but in everything by prayer and supplication I will let my requests be made known unto you. As I do so, I know that your supernatural peace that surpasses all understanding will keep my heart and my mind through Jesus Christ. Thank you, Father.

Through your grace I will remain focused on the things that are true, honest, just, pure, lovely, and of good report. I will think on these things, and all mental confusion I have been experiencing will be gone. Hallelujah!

Direct me, Father, as I place my full trust in you. Let me never experience confusion again. Deliver me in your righteousness and help me to escape from any confusion. During the time when confusion was continually before me, the shame of my face covered me. Now, however, I am free because you have delivered me. Hallelujah!

Help me, Father, to practice and demonstrate good works. May I never engage in bitter envying and strife in my heart. I know that envying and strife lead to confusion and every evil work. Therefore, I will put those things behind me, realizing that your wisdom is pure, peaceable, gentle, easy to be entreated, full of mercy and good fruits, without partiality, and without hypocrisy. I will walk in your wisdom, Lord, for I know that's the pathway of peace. May I never forget that the fruit of righteousness is sown in peace by them that make peace. Help me to be a peacemaker at all times, I pray.

Because I believe in Jesus Christ as my Savior and Lord, I know I shall never be confounded or confused. Thank you, Father. I know that the natural man is unable to receive the things of the Spirit of God because they are foolishness unto him and he cannot discern them. He who is spiritual, however, has the mind of Christ and is able to discern spiritual things.

Thank you, Lord, for renewing me in the spirit of my mind and lifting me above all confusion. I put on the new man, which is created in righteousness and true holiness. Putting all mental confusion behind me, along with lying, I will speak truth with everyone. I will not sin through anger nor will I let the sun go down upon my wrath. I will give no place to the devil ever again.

In Jesus' name I pray, Amen.

Scriptures: 1 Corinthians 14:33; Philippians 4:6-7; Philippians 4:8; Proverbs 3:5-6; Psalm 71:1; Psalm 44:15; James 3:14-18; 1 Peter 2:6; 1 Corinthians 2:14-16; Ephesians 4:23-27.

Personal Affirmation: I will abide in Christ and let His words abide in me. (See John 15:4.) If I abide in Him and His words abide in me, I will ask what I will and I know it will be done for me. (See John 15:7.) As I apply these truths to my life, all mental confusion is gone. Praise the Lord!

Reflection: *"God has a plan for your life. The enemy has a plan for your life. Be ready for both and wise enough to know the difference"* (Author unknown).

24

Newness of Life

Therefore if any man be in Christ, he is a new creature: old things are passed away; behold, all things are become new.

(2 CORINTHIANS 5:17)

Central Focus: Someone has aptly stated that Christianity is the land of new beginnings. Yes, every day is a new beginning in Jesus. He makes all things new. The moment when we receive Him as our Savior we experience newness of life, for we are born again into His marvelous kingdom.

Prayer: Dear Lord, thank you for the newness of life you've given to me through Jesus Christ, my Lord. He is the King of kings and the Lord of lords. It is wonderful to know that I was buried with Him by baptism into death, that in the same manner that Christ was raised from the dead by your glory, Father, just so am I able to walk in newness of life. What a joy this newness of life is!

I waited patiently for you, O Lord, and you inclined your ear unto me and heard my cry. You brought me out of a horrible pit, out of the miry clay, and you set my feet upon a rock and established all my goings. Thank you for putting a new song in my mouth, even a song of praise to you.

I delight to do your will, O my God, and your law is within my heart. Thank you for casting away all my transgressions and giving me a new heart and a new spirit. I know I am being renewed in the spirit of my mind and that I am putting on the new man, which after you has been created in righteousness and true holiness.

Heavenly Father, I want to follow you in all things, as your dear child. Therefore, I determine to walk in love, as Christ has loved me and has given himself as a sacrifice for my sins. Thank you for giving me the grace to put on the new man, which is renewed in knowledge after your image, Father.

I bless you, Lord. All that is within me blesses your holy name. I will never forget all your benefits to me. You have forgiven all my iniquities and healed all my diseases. You have redeemed my life from destruction and have crowned me with tender mercies. Thank you for satisfying my mouth with good things so that my youth is renewed like the eagle's.

Create in me a clean heart, O God; and renew a right spirit within me. Cast me not away from your presence, and do not take your Holy Spirit away from me. Restore unto me the joy of your salvation, and uphold me with your free Spirit.

Though my outward man may be perishing, I know that my inner self is being renewed every day. Thank you, Father, for allowing me to walk in newness of life. By your mercies to me, dear Father, I now present my body as a living sacrifice to you, for I realize this is my reasonable service to you. Keep me from ever being conformed to this world, but to be transformed by the renewing of my mind so that I will be able to prove what is your good, acceptable, and perfect will.

In the power of Jesus' name I pray, Amen.

Scriptures: Deuteronomy 10:17; Romans 6:4; Psalm 40:1-2; Psalm 40:8; Ezekiel 36:26; Ephesians 4:23-24; Ephesians 5:1-2; Colossians 3:10: Psalm 101:1-4; Psalm 31:10:12; 2 Corinthians 4:16; Romans 12:1-2.

Personal Affirmation: As I walk in newness of life each day, everything takes on a bright and fresh aspect that gives me joy and hope. God has made me into an entirely new person!

Reflection: *"We are blood-secured, delivered from the enemy's power, and raised up into newness of life in God"* (David Wilkerson).

25

Overwrought

*I have set the Lord always before me:
because he is at my right hand, I shall not
be moved. Therefore my heart is glad, and
my glory rejoiceth; my flesh also shall rest in
hope.*

(PSALM 16:9)

Central Focus: To be overwrought is to be
overworked, worried, and fatigued. It involves being
nervous and excited. God does not want His people
to be overwrought. He wants us to learn to rest in
Him and in His hope.

Prayer: Father, this sense of being overwrought has
come about because I've been doing so much in my
own strength. Your Word teaches me that without
you I can do nothing, and it assures me that I can
do all things through Christ who strengthens me.
Forgive me for failing you in this, Lord, for I know I
need your help in all that I do.

I ask you, Father, to restore unto me the years that the cankerworm and the palmerworm have destroyed. Thank you for sending Jesus to give me life and that more abundantly. Thank you for the peace Jesus has given unto me. Thank you for restoring physical and emotional health to me.

I wait upon you, O Lord, and as I do so, I know you are renewing my strength. I am mounting up with wings as eagles, and I am running without being weary and walking without fainting. I praise you for every promise of your Word.

I love you, O Lord, my strength. You are my rock, my fortress, and my deliverer. You are my God and my strength, and I will always trust in you. You are my buckler, the horn of my salvation, and my high tower. I will call upon you, for you are worthy to be praised. In this way I know you will deliver me from this constant feeling of being overwrought and overburdened. Thank you, Father.

I am so grateful for your promise to keep me in perfect peace as I keep my mind stayed on you and trust in you. Through your grace I will be anxious for nothing, but in everything by prayer and supplication with thanksgiving I will let my requests be made known to you. As I do so, I know that your peace, which surpasses all understanding, will guard my heart and my mind through Christ Jesus.

Help me to become complete in you, Father, and to be of good comfort, single-minded, and dwelling in peace. I know that you, the God of love and peace, will always be with me. This fact alone alleviates all the stress, anxiety, pressure, and fatigue I've been experiencing.

In Jesus' name I pray, Amen.

Scriptures: John 15:5; Philippians 4:13; Joel 1:4; John 10:10; John 14:27; Isaiah 40:31; Psalm 18:1-3; Isaiah 26:3; Philippians 4:6-7; 2 Corinthians 13:11.

Personal Affirmation: I am no longer overwrought, because God's peace has filled me to overflowing. His peace is absolutely perfect.

Reflection: *"God, you have made us for yourself, and our hearts are restless till they find their rest in thee"* (St. Augustine).

26

Physical Pain

Jesus Christ is the same yesterday, today, and forever.

(HEBREWS 13:8)

Central Focus: Pain involves strong discomfort and great suffering. Jesus is the Great Physician of our souls and bodies, and we need to go to Him when we are feeling pain. "More things are wrought by prayer than this world dreams of" (Alfred, Lord Tennyson), and when we are in pain we need to pray and seek God's comfort and healing power.

Prayer: Heavenly Father, I thank you for Jesus who bore my sins in His own body on the tree, that I might live for righteousness. It is by His stripes that I am healed of this pain and sickness. He forgives all my iniquities and heals all my diseases and pain. I believe, Lord, that you want me to prosper in all things and enjoy good health.

The Bible says that Jesus is the same yesterday, today, and forever. I believe this truth with all my heart, and because I do, I know that He is still the healer. When He walked upon this Earth, He went about all the cities and villages, teaching in their synagogues, preaching the gospel of the Kingdom, and healing every sickness and disease among the people. May His healing power take away my pain.

He was wounded for my transgressions. He was bruised for my iniquities. The chastisement for my peace was upon Him, and by His stripes I am healed. Thank you, Father, for this promise and for all the promises of your Word, which are yes and amen in Christ Jesus.

I will give full attention to your Word and I will incline my ear to your sayings. I will not let them depart from my eyes. I will keep them in the midst of my heart, for I know that they are life and health to all my flesh. Praise your name, Lord.

As I reach out to you, Father, I pray in faith, for I know that the prayer of faith will save me from pain and you will raise me up. Thank you, Lord. I will diligently heed your voice and do what is right in your sight. I will give ear to your commandments and keep all your statutes. Thank you for assuring me that you want health for me. I know you are the Lord who heals me.

As I pray, I believe you are restoring health to me and healing me of all my wounds and pain. Hallelujah! Heal me, O Lord, and I shall be healed. Save me, and

I shall be saved, for you are my praise. Send your Word, Father, and heal me and deliver me from pain.

In the name of Jesus, my Healer, I pray, Amen.

Scriptures: 1 Peter 2:24; 3 John 2; Hebrews 13:8; Matthew 9:35; Luke 6:19; Isaiah 53:5; 2 Corinthians 1:20; Proverbs 4:20-22; James 5:14-15; Exodus 15:26; Jeremiah 30:17; Jeremiah 17:14; Psalm 107:20.

Personal Affirmation: God is my Healer. I will always trust in Him. It is my firm belief that He is taking my pain away, and I look forward to being completely pain-free in the near future. All power belongs to Him, and He is able to do exceedingly abundantly beyond all that I could ever ask or think, according to the power that works within me. (See Ephesians 3:20.) Unto Him be glory in the Church by Christ Jesus throughout all ages, world without end. (See Ephesians 3:21.)

Reflection: *"I am not a theologian or a scholar, but I am very aware of the fact that pain is necessary to all of us. In my own life, I think I can honestly say that out of the deepest pain has come the strongest conviction of the presence of God and the love of God"* (Elisabeth Elliot).

27

Passivity

You shall walk after the Lord your God and fear Him, and keep his commandments and obey His voice; you shall serve Him and hold fast to Him.

(DEUTERONOMY 13:4 NKJV)

Central Focus: Christian believers are agents of change in the world. They should always be active in their service to the Lord and others. To be passive is to be inactive. A passive person is acted upon by circumstances and other people and rarely takes action to improve those circumstances. The passive person, in other words, offers little or no resistance to the forces that come against him or her.

Prayer: Father God, I ask that you would help me to be always confident in you. With your help I will be steadfast, immoveable, and always abounding in your work, for I know that my labor will never be in vain when it is in you, my Lord and my God. By your mercies to me, I present my body as a living sacrifice unto you—holy and acceptable unto you, because I know this is my reasonable service. I will not allow myself to be conformed to this world any longer, because I know you are transforming me through the renewal of my mind so that I may prove what your perfect will is.

Help me, Lord, to be kindly affectionate toward others with brotherly kindness. I desire to walk in love and honor and I want to give preference to others and I never want to lag in diligence. Instead, through your Spirit I will be fervent in spirit, as I serve you. I will distribute to the saints and practice hospitality.

Father, I will attend to your Word and incline my ear to your sayings. I will not let them depart from my eyes. I will keep them in the midst of my heart, for I know they are life and health to me. Thank you, Father. Through your grace I will keep my heart with all diligence, for I know the very issues of life stem from my heart.

Thank you for enabling me to abound in everything, including faith, utterance, knowledge, diligence, and love. Father, I want my love to be active, as I reach out to those in need. Show me how to bear the burdens of others so that I would always fulfill your law. Teach me to respond proactively when I see any need in others or myself.

It thrills me to know, Lord, that you will not forget my labors of love. Help me always to minister to the saints and to show diligence in my work to the full assurance of hope until the end. I choose not to be passive or slothful, and I will be a follower of those who, through faith and patience, inherit your promises. Thank you, Father.

I will be your diligent servant, Lord, and I will give diligence to make my calling and election sure. By so doing, I know I can never fail. Hallelujah!

In the name of the Lord Jesus I pray, Amen.

Scriptures: 1 John 2:28; 1 Corinthians 15:58; Romans 12:1-2; Romans 12:10-11, 13; Proverbs 4:20-23; 2 Corinthians 8:7; Galatians 6:2; Hebrews 6:11-12; 2 Peter 1:10.

Personal Affirmation: I choose to be a hard-working ambassador for my Lord and Savior, Jesus Christ. I want to serve Him always with my whole heart. I will keep His precepts diligently. (See Psalm 119:4.) As I put all passivity, laziness, and sloth behind me, I know that I will be fruitful in every good work. I will walk worthy of the Lord unto all pleasing. I will be a fruit-bearing Christian, as I increase in my knowledge of God. (See Colossians 1:10.)

Reflection: *"God's work done in God's way will never lack God's supplies"* (Hudson Taylor).

28

People-pleasing

When a man's ways please the Lord, He makes even his enemies be at peace with him.

(PROVERBS 16:7 NKJV)

Central Focus: Pleasing God must always take priority over pleasing people. Too often a people-pleaser is someone who fears others, or at least fears displeasing them. God does not want you to fear others. In fact, He has given His love to you, and His love casts out all fear. (See 1 John 4:18.)

Prayer: Without faith, it is impossible to please you, Lord, for he who comes to you must believe that you exist and that you are a rewarder of them that diligently seek you. Father, I will always seek you diligently. Help me to remember that I can never please you if I am operating in the flesh and that when my focus is on pleasing others I am operating in the flesh. Help me to remember that I am not in the flesh, but in the Spirit. He dwells within me. Praise His holy name!

Do I seek to please people or you, Father? If I seek to please people, I should not be the servant of Christ, and I want to be His servant at all times. I want to always put you first, Father, as I seek first your kingdom and your righteousness. How I praise you for your promise that you will add all things unto me as I do so. Help me to abound more and more in my efforts to please you, Lord.

Through your power I will be strong in the grace that is in Christ Jesus. The things that I have heard from you I will commit to the faithful, and they will be able to teach others also. Help me to endure hardness, Father, as a good servant of Jesus Christ, for I know this will please you.

God, I ask that you would fill me with the knowledge of your will in all wisdom and spiritual understanding. It is my desire to walk worthy of you and to be fruitful in every good work, as I increase in my knowledge of you. Strengthen me with all might, according to your glorious power, with all patience and longsuffering with joyfulness.

I give thanks to you, Father, for you have made it possible for me to be a partaker of the inheritance of the saints in light. You have delivered me from the power of darkness, and you have translated me into the Kingdom of your dear Son in whom I have redemption through His blood, even the forgiveness of my sins. Help me always to keep my focus on pleasing you, Lord.

Thank you, Father, for entrusting me with the gospel. I will proclaim the good news to others, not as pleasing people, but as pleasing you. Putting you first, Father, I know that my heart will no longer condemn me. I have great confidence in you. Therefore, I know that I will receive whatever I ask of you, because I keep your commandments and do those things that are pleasing in your sight. I want this to be the theme of my life always—to put your first and to please you—instead of pleasing people.

From now on, my focus will be on pleasing you, Lord. I do not want to be a people-pleaser, but I do want to love others in word and in deed.

Thank you, Lord God, for enabling me to be a God-pleaser instead of a people-pleaser.

In Jesus' name I pray, Amen.

Scriptures: Hebrews 11:6; Romans 8:8-9; Galatians 1:10; Matthew 6:33; 1 Thessalonians 4:1; 2 Timothy 2:1-3; Colossians 1:9-14; 1 Thessalonians 1:4; 1 John 3:22; 1 John 3:18.

Personal Affirmation: People-pleasing is a form of weakness that I want nothing to do with. I will keep my focus on pleasing God at all times. How do I please Him? By obedience to Him and His Word. There is great disappointment in trying to please others, but there is great reward in pleasing God. The Bible says, There is no fear in love; but perfect love casts out fear, because fear involves torment. But he who fears has not been made perfect in love. (1 John 4:18 NKJV.)

Reflection: *"You don't have to please others. Just do what God wants you to do, because at the end of the day, it is only He who can satisfy your heart. Not the approval or applause from other people"* (Author unknown).

29

Phobias

There is no fear in love; but perfect love casteth out fear; because fear hath torment. He that feareth is not made perfect in love.

(1 JOHN 4:18)

Central Focus: Phobias are irrational fears that torment those who have them. God does not want His people to fear anyone or anything. It is through faith and trust that we are delivered from phobias and fears in any form. We must remember that God has not given us a spirit of fear, but of power and love and of a sound mind. (See 2 Timothy 1:7.)

Prayer: Abba-Father, thank you for adopting me into your family. I know I have not received the spirit of bondage again to fear, but I have received the Spirit of adoption that enables me to cry out to you, "Abba-Father."

Thank you so much for your promise to cover me with your feathers. Under your wings I take refuge. Your truth is my shield and buckler. Therefore, I will not be afraid of the terror by night nor of the arrow that flies by day. I will not fear the pestilence that walks in darkness, nor the destruction that lays waste at noonday. I know that a thousand may fall at my side and ten thousand at my right hand, but these things will not come near me. For this I thank you so much, dear God.

Your Word declares that no evil shall befall me and no plague shall come near my dwelling. Thank you so much for giving your angels charge over me. I know they will keep me in all my ways. Hallelujah!

I am so thankful to know that phobias will not haunt me any longer. I will not be afraid of sudden terror or of trouble from the wicked when it comes. Lord God, I know you will always be my confidence and you will keep my foot from being caught. I will be established in righteousness and I will always be far from oppression. Therefore, I will not fear, for I know that terror shall not come near to me.

I have put my trust in you, Father. Therefore, I will no longer be afraid. What can others do to me? Yea, though I walk through the valley of the shadow of death, I will fear no evil, for I know you are with me. I know that your rod and staff will protect me. Thank you for preparing a table for me in the presence of my enemies and for anointing my head with oil. My cup truly overflows.

I will be of good courage, and I know you will strengthen my heart, as I hope in you. You have delivered me from the phobias of my past. You are my helper. I will not fear any longer. Hallelujah! You are my light and my salvation. Whom shall I fear? You are the strength of my life. Of what shall I be afraid? Though an army encamps against me, my heart will not fear. Though wars arise against me, I will be confident in you.

I will always dwell in your secret place, O Most High. I will always abide under your shadow, Almighty God.

Thank you for delivering me from the phobias I've dealt with for so long.

In Jesus' name I pray, Amen.

Scriptures: Romans 8:15; Psalm 91:4-7; Psalm 91:10-11; Proverbs 3:25-26; Isaiah 54:14; Psalm 56:11; Psalm 23:4-5; Psalm 31:24; Psalm 91:1.

Personal Affirmation: God has delivered me from all phobias. Therefore, I will rejoice in Him. He is my refuge and strength, and a very present help in times of trouble. Therefore, I will not fear. The Lord of hosts is with me, and the God of Jacob is my refuge. (See Psalm 46.)

Reflection: *"Prayer in the sense of petition, asking for things, is a small part of it; confession and penitence are its threshold, adoration its sanctuary, the presence and enjoyment of God its bread and wine"* (C.S. Lewis).

30

Promises of God

By which have been given to us exceedingly great and precious promises, that through these you may be partakers of the divine nature, having escaped the corruption that is in the world through lust.

(2 PETER 1:4 NKJV)

Central Focus: There are approximately 7000 promises in God's Word, and these are for us to claim and appropriate for our own lives. God promises so much to each of us, and we can count on Him to fulfill His promises in our lives. However, some promises are conditional, and one of those conditions is obedience. As we learn to obey the Lord and trust Him, we will see His promises coming true in our lives.

Prayer: O God, my heavenly Father, thank you for every one of your great and precious promises. I believe them, receive them, and take action upon them. You are the great Promise-keeper, and I am blessed to be a promise-reaper.

Father, I know that all your promises in Christ Jesus are yes and in Him amen. Thank you for each of your promises. Thank you for establishing me and anointing me. Having, therefore, these wonderful promises, I choose to cleanse myself from all filthiness of the flesh and spirit. Help me to perfect my life in holiness and in the fear of you.

Help me never to be slothful. I want to be a follower of those who through faith and patience inherit your promises. Thank you, Abba-Father, for giving me a blessed inheritance and for predestinating me, according to your purposes. Thank you, Lord, for the exceeding greatness of your power that has come to me through faith, according to the working of your mighty power.

I know that you are never slack concerning your promises, Father, and I thank you also that you are not willing that any should perish, but that all should come to repentance. It is my desire to be like Abraham who against hope believed in hope, that he might become the father of many nations. He did not waver at your promise through unbelief, but he was strong in faith, giving glory unto you. Like Abraham, I am fully persuaded that you are able to perform what you have promised to me.

I know you cannot lie, dear Father. You are always faithful to me and you will always be faithful to fulfill your promises in my life. I put my hope in your promises. I know your compassion toward me will never fail. Your mercies are new every morning. Great is your faithfulness, O God. You are my portion, and I will always hope in you.

Your mercies, dear God, reach to the heavens and your faithfulness reaches to the skies. How excellent is your lovingkindness. Therefore, I put my trust under the shadow of your wings, and I will completely trust in you. I will do good, and I know you will take care of me. I delight myself in you and your promises, and I know you will give me the desires of my heart. I commit my way to you, as I trust in you, and I know you will bring it to pass.

I will walk upon your promises, Father, for they truly are steppingstones to a fuller life. Thank you so much for blessing me in so many ways.

In Jesus' name I pray, Amen.

Scriptures: 2 Corinthians 1:20-21; 2 Corinthians 7:1; Hebrews 6:12; Ephesians 1:11; Ephesians 1:19; 2 Peter 3:9; Romans 4:16-21; Titus 1:2; Lamentations 3:21-24; Psalm 36:5-7; Psalm 37:2-5.

Personal Affirmation: God's promises to me are like apples on a tree. All I have to do is reach out and take them. This I will do each day of my life, and I know His blessings will always be there for me. The Bible says, "And all these blessings shall come on thee, and overtake thee, if thou shalt hearken unto the voice of the Lord thy God" (Deuteronomy 28:2).

Reflection: *"Let God's promises shine on your problems"* (Corrie ten Boom).

31

Quietness

In quietness and in confidence shall be your strength.

(ISAIAH 30:15)

Central Focus: God wants us to still our hearts and experience Him. (See Psalm 46:10.) To be still is to be restful and peaceful. To be quiet is to be undistracted by noise or any other thing. God wants us to rest in Him. David wrote, "The Lord is my shepherd; I shall not want. He maketh me to lie down in green pastures; he leadeth me beside the still waters. He restoreth my soul" (Psalm 23:1-3.) Notice from the preceding Scripture that the restoration of our souls comes when we take our rest in the green pastures He provides for us, and as our souls are restored, we gain strength to face the battles of our lives.

Prayer: Lord God, I will rest in you and wait patiently for you. I will not worry any longer. I will be quiet both on the inside and the outside. My Lord Jesus promises me, "Come unto me, all you that labor and are heavy laden, and I will give you rest. Take my yoke upon you, and learn of me; for I am meek and lowly in heart: and ye shall find rest unto your souls. For my yoke is easy, and my burden is light." Thank you, Jesus, for the rest you provide for me.

Lord God, you are my keeper and the shade upon my right hand. The sun shall not smite me by day nor the moon by night. Thank you for your promise to preserve me from all evil. I know you will preserve my soul and my going out and my coming in from this time forth and forevermore. Hallelujah!

In your presence, Father, there is fullness of joy and there are pleasures forevermore. I know your presence will go with me, and you will give me rest. Thank you so much for the rest and peace I find in your presence, as I am quiet before you.

With deep certainty I know that all things work together for good in my life, because I love you and you have called me according to your purpose. Thank you for justifying me by faith and giving me peace with you through my Lord Jesus Christ. It is by Him that I have access to your grace and I am able to rejoice in hope of your glory, Father.

It is wonderful to know that you will keep me in perfect peace as I stay my mind on you and trust you completely. Teach me how not to be anxious, Father, but in everything by prayer and supplication, with thanksgiving, I will let my requests be made known unto you. As I do so, your wonderful peace, which surpasses all understanding, will guard my heart and my mind through Christ Jesus.

Through your grace I will let your peace rule in my heart, and I will be thankful. Thank you for giving me your peace and strength. I will lie down in peace and quietness and sleep, for you alone make me to dwell in safety.

In Jesus' name I pray, Amen.

Scriptures: Psalm 37:7; Matthew 11:28-30; Psalm 121:5-8; Psalm 16:11; Exodus 33:14; Romans 8:28; Romans 5:1-2; Isaiah 26:3; Philippians 4:6-7; Colossians 3:15; Psalm 29:11; Psalm 4:8.

Personal Affirmation: As I quiet myself in God's presence, I hear His voice speaking to me, and I know He loves me with an everlasting love. I will seek quietness and peace at every opportunity. I will be still and draw close to God. Putting all anxiety behind me, I will rest in the Lord. He is my everlasting portion.

Reflection: *"Each time, before you intercede, be quiet first, and worship God in His glory. Think of what He can do, and how He delights to hear the prayers of His redeemed people. Think of your place and privilege in Christ, and expect great things!"* (Andrew Murray).

32

Restlessness

Therefore my heart is glad, and my glory rejoices: my flesh also will rest in hope.

(PSALM 16:9 NKJV)

Central Focus: Restlessness is the opposite of rest. If we are restless, we are failing to avail ourselves of the rest God has provided for His people. (See Hebrews 4:9.) As we learn to rest in the Lord, all pressure, anxiety, and stress evaporate, and we find a whole new approach to life. This is God's will for us. He never wants us to be restless. He is our peace and we find our rest in Him.

Prayer: Teach me, Lord, to trust in you and do good. As I learn to do so, I know I shall dwell in the land and be fed. I will delight myself in you, and I know you will give me the desires of my heart. I will commit my way unto you and trust completely in you, and I know you will give answers to my prayers and bring forth your righteousness as the light and your judgment as the noonday. Knowing these truths, I will rest in you, Lord, and wait patiently for you.

Realizing how bountifully you have dealt with me, Father, my soul shall return unto the rest you have provided for me. Thank you so much for your rest. You have delivered my soul from death, my eyes from tears, and my feet from falling. Therefore, I will walk before you in the land of the living.

One of the causes for restlessness is anxiety, and I now realize that I do not need to be anxious about anything. I will cast all my cares upon you, O Lord, for I know you care for me. I cast my burden upon you, and I know you will sustain me. Thank you, Father.

Your wonderful grace is sufficient for me, Father, and your strength is made perfect in my weakness. I ask that you let the power of Christ rest upon me. Thank you, Father, for your promise to let me enter your rest. I will always endeavor to enter your rest. Through your grace I will come boldly unto your throne of grace, that I may obtain mercy and find grace to help me in my time of need.

Be pleased, O Lord, to deliver me from all restlessness, and make haste to help me. O Lord my God, I put my trust in you. Deliver me from restlessness and set me free. Thank you for the Holy Spirit, my Comforter. I rejoice in the knowledge that He will teach me all things and bring all things to my remembrance. The peace of Jesus will be with me forever. Therefore, I will not ever need to be restless again.

Father, I thank you for your Word. Teach me to always keep your commandments, for I know that as I do so, you will give me long life and peace. Thank you, Father, for being rich in mercy and for your great love with which you have loved me. Christ Jesus is my peace. He has broken down the middle wall of partition. Thank you, Lord, for your peace which surpasses all understanding and sets me free from all restlessness.

Through your grace I will be strong in you and in the power of your might.

In Jesus' name I pray, Amen.

Scriptures: Psalm 37:3-7; Psalm 116:7-9; Philippians 4:6; 1 Peter 5:7; Psalm 55:22; 2 Corinthians 12:9; Hebrews 4; Psalm 40:13; Psalm 7:1; John 14:27; Proverbs 3:1-2; Ephesians 2:4; Ephesians 2:14; Philippians 4:7; Ephesians 6:10.

Personal Affirmation: Restlessness has been my enemy for far too long, but God has delivered me from it and I am now experiencing His wonderful peace and joy. I will remember that my Father is not the author of restlessness, but of peace. I will walk in His peace and joy from this time forth.

Reflection: *"Pay attention to your restlessness. Sometimes it's God's way of redirecting you"* (Author unknown).

33

Righteousness

For he hath made him to be sin for us, who knew no sin; that we might be made the righteousness of God in him.

(2 CORINTHIANS 5:21)

Central Focus: We cannot attain to any righteousness without the Lord Jesus Christ who is our righteousness. Righteousness involves acting in a just, upright manner. It leads us to always do what is right. To be righteous is to be morally right, fair, and just. These attributes come to us only as we yield completely to Jesus Christ.

Prayer: Thank you, Father, for sending Jesus. He became wisdom, righteousness, sanctification, and redemption, and He lives within me. This means I possess all those qualities in my own spirit, and this is wonderful knowledge indeed. Help me to walk in wisdom, righteousness, sanctification, and redemption throughout my life.

May I ever be found in Him, not having my own righteousness, which is from the Law, but that which is through faith in Christ—the righteousness which is from you by faith. Thank you for justifying me freely by your grace through the redemption that is in Christ Jesus. Thank you, Father, for sending Jesus forth as a propitiation for my sins by His blood, through faith, to demonstrate your righteousness.

Because I know I have received abundance of grace and the gift of righteousness, I know I shall reign through my Lord Jesus Christ. I praise you, Father, that you are establishing me in righteousness. Therefore, I shall be far from all oppression and fear. I know that no weapon which is formed against me shall prosper, and I know that you will condemn every tongue which rises against me, for this is the heritage of your servants, and their righteousness is from you. Thank you, Father.

The work of righteousness in my life is peace, and the effects of righteousness are quietness and assurance forever. With my heart, I believe unto righteousness and with my mouth I make confession unto salvation. According to your mercy you saved me through the washing of regeneration and renewing of the Holy Spirit. Thank you, Father.

Hear me when I call, O God of my righteousness. You have enlarged me when I was in distress. Have mercy upon me, and hear my prayer. Through your righteousness, I will be able to approve things that are excellent, that I may be sincere and without offense until the day of Christ. Fill me with the fruits of righteousness, which are by Jesus Christ, unto your glory and praise, Father.

With your help, I will flee from everything that is evil and I will follow after righteousness, godliness, faith, love, patience, and meekness. I will fight the good fight of faith, as I lay hold on eternal life to which you have called me.

Help me to be like Abraham, Father, who believed you, and his faith was imputed unto him as righteousness. He was called your friend. Increase my faith, Lord, and help me to grow in my relationship with you.

In Jesus' name I pray, Amen.

Scriptures: 1 Corinthians 1:30; Romans 3:24; Romans 5:17; Isaiah 54:14-17; Isaiah 32:17; Romans 10:10; Titus 3:5; Psalm 4:1; Philippians 1:10-11; 1 Timothy 6:11-12; James 2:23.

Personal Affirmation: All of my righteousness is as filthy rags in the sight of God. (See Isaiah 64:6.) The only kind of righteousness I can have on my own is self-righteousness, and I want all self-righteousness to be gone from my life. Instead, I will draw close to God, and I know He will impute His righteousness to me. The Kingdom of God is within me, and His Kingdom is not meat and drink, but righteousness, peace, and joy in the Holy Spirit. I thank God for the work of His righteousness in my life.

Reflection: *"If we walk in righteousness, He will carry us through"* (A.B. Simpson).

34

Sarcasm

Let all bitterness, wrath, anger, clamor, and evil speaking be put away from you, with all malice. And be kind to one another, tenderhearted, forgiving one another, even as God in Christ forgave you.

(EPHESIANS 4:31-32 NKJV)

Central Focus: Sarcasm is a work of the flesh that is often harmful to others. It involves taunting, sneering, cutting, and caustic remarks. A person with a sarcastic attitude cannot be an effective witness for Jesus Christ. We need to learn to replace all sarcasm with the fruit of God's Holy Spirit: love, joy, peace, patience, gentleness, goodness, faith, meekness, and self-control. (See Galatians 5:22-23.) Be filled with God's Holy Spirit, and there will be no room for sarcasm any more.

Prayer: Heavenly Father, I repent of my attitude of sarcasm. I never want to hurt others. Help me to control my tongue, for I realize that death and life are in the power of my tongue, and I never want to injure others by speaking sarcastically to them or about them. Through the power of your Holy Spirit I will let no corrupt communication proceed out of my mouth, but that which is good to the use of edifying, that it may minister grace to everyone who hears me.

Help me to remember that pleasant words are as a honeycomb, for they are sweet to the soul and they are health to my bones. I want to speak only pleasant words at all times. Help me to keep guard over my mouth, because I know that those who open wide their lips are on the path to destruction. Lord, it is sobering to know that one day I shall have to give an account to you for every idle word I speak.

Thank you for showing me that foolish questions, contentions, and strivings about the Law are to be avoided, for they are both unprofitable and vain. I love life, Father, and I want to see good days, so I will refrain from all sarcasm and evil speaking. My lips will not speak guile any longer. I believe your Word which tells me that a wholesome tongue is a tree of life.

As James points out, the tongue is a fire and a world of iniquity. The tongue can defile my whole body, and it sets on fire the course of nature. I realize that both blessing and cursing should not come from the same mouth. Set a watch, O Lord, before my mouth, and keep the door of my lips.

Keep me from all sarcasm, Father, for I know that sarcastic speech can be like the piercing of a sword, but the tongue of the wise is health. Thank you for calling me Father. I want to follow you in all things and to be holy in all my conversation.

With your help I will guard the words of my mouth and tongue and thereby keep my soul from troubles. Help me to speak forth your Word and your will at all times and to talk about Jesus whenever I have the opportunity to do so.

In Jesus' name I pray, Amen.

Scriptures: Proverbs 18:21; Ephesians 4:29; Proverbs 16:24; Proverbs 13:3; Matthew 12:36; Titus 3:9; 1 Peter 3:10; Proverbs 15:4; James 3:6, 10-11; Psalm 141:3; Proverbs 12:18-19; 1 Peter 1:15; Proverbs 21:23.

Personal Affirmation: The gift of speech is a sacred trust and it must be used with wisdom and compassion at all times. I will keep my speech positive and brief, realizing that in the multitude of words there is sin. (See Proverbs 10:19.) I will let my speech always be seasoned with grace and salt, so that I will always know how to answer every person. (See Colossians 4:6.)

Reflection: *"Live in such a way that those who know you, but don't know God, will come to know God because they know you"* (Author unknown).

35

Seeking God

O God, You are my God; early will I seek you; my soul thirsts for You; my flesh longs for You in a dry and thirsty land where there is no water. So I have looked for You in the sanctuary, to see Your power and Your glory. Because Your lovingkindness is better than life, my lips shall praise You.

(PSALM 63:1-3 NKJV)

Central Focus: We are able to seek God through prayer, His Word, worship, and Christian fellowship. To seek Him means to earnestly search for Him until we find Him. The Bible shows us that He wants us to seek Him and to follow Him. So seek the Lord while He may be found. As you do so, He will seek your good. (See Psalm 122:9.)

Prayer: O Lord, I seek first your kingdom and your righteousness, and I know that as I do so, I will find you and you will bless me abundantly. I seek you and your strength, Lord. I will seek your face forevermore and remember your marvelous works and wonders.

You are the Lord my God. Hallelujah!

Father, I will seek you early each day, and I know I shall find you. Thank you for imparting your spiritual understanding to me as I seek you. I will seek you in meekness, Lord, and I will also seek your righteousness. As I ask, I know it shall be given unto me. As I knock, I know it will be opened, and as I seek, I know I shall find. Thank you, Father, for these promises from your Word. Seeking you is life's greatest adventure, and finding you is life's greatest joy.

Help me to grow in the grace and knowledge of my Lord Jesus Christ. I will meditate upon your words of truth. As I seek you, Father, I know you are filling me with the knowledge of your will in all wisdom and spiritual understanding. This will enable me to walk worthy of you, fully pleasing you, and to be fruitful in every good work as I increase in my knowledge of you. Thank you for strengthening me with all might, according to your glorious power, for all patience and longsuffering with joy.

Thank you for dealing well with me, Lord, and for enabling me to find you. You always deal with me according to your Word. You are always faithful to me, and you fulfill your promises in my life. Thank you, Lord. You are my God forever and ever, and you will be my guide unto death.

I will trust in you with all my heart and not lean upon my own understanding. In all my ways I will acknowledge you, and I know you will always direct my steps. You are near to me as I seek you and call upon you in truth. Thank you for your promise to fulfill my desires, to hear my cry, and to save me.

I come boldly to your throne of grace, knowing that I will obtain mercy and find grace to help me in my time of need. Thank you, Father, for helping me to find you and to abide in you.

In Jesus' name I pray, Amen.

Scriptures: Matthew 6:33; Psalm 105:4-7; Proverbs 8:17; Proverbs 28:5; Zephaniah 2:3; Matthew 7:7; 2 Peter 3:18; 1 Timothy 4:15; Colossians 1:9-11; Psalm 119:65; 1 Thessalonians 5:24; Psalm 48:14; Proverbs 3:5-6; Psalm 145:18-19; Hebrews 4:14.

Personal Affirmation: I sought the Lord, and He heard me. Now I know He is with me, and I will walk in His love and presence each step of my way. A great saint once said, "The greatest romance is loving God, the greatest adventure is seeking Him, and the greatest joy is finding Him." Now that I've found the Lord, I will stay close to Him always.

Reflection: *"I feel it is far better to begin with God, to see His face first, to get my soul near Him before it is near another. In general, it is best to have at least one hour alone with God before engaging in anything else"* (E. M. Bounds).

36

Self-importance

Be clothed with humility, for God resists the proud, but give graces to the humble. Therefore humble yourselves under the mighty hand of God that He may exalt you in due time.

(1 PETER 5:5-6 NKJV)

Central Focus: Self-importance stems from an exaggerated opinion of oneself. A self-important person is one who is pompous, arrogant, and officious. God clearly wants His people to humble themselves under His mighty hand, to be clothed with humility, and to resist pride. We can accomplish these changes through His grace, which is always sufficient for us. (See 2 Corinthians 12:9.)

Prayer: Heavenly Father, help me never to think of myself more highly than I ought to think, but to think soberly. I respectfully fear you, Lord, and I hate evil. I also hate pride, arrogance, and every evil way. Help me, Lord, to walk away from such things and to humble myself before you. I want all self-importance to go.

Help me to remember that pride goes before destruction and a haughty spirit before a fall. Keep me from falling and from all destruction I pray, I choose to be of a humble spirit with the lowly instead of dividing the spoil with the proud. I know that self-importance and pride will bring me low, so I will avoid them with all my heart, because I know honor will uphold all who are humble in heart. Help me to be humble in my heart, Lord.

Through your grace, I will never love the world, nor the things that are in the world, because I know that when I love the world, I turn my back on your love. All that is in the world—the lust of the flesh, the lust of the eyes, and the pride of life—is not of you, Father. They are of the world, and I want to avoid all forms of worldliness at all times.

I realize, Lord, that I stir up strife when I act in self-important ways. I would far rather trust in you with a humble heart. I know you never forget the cry of the humble, Lord. Help me always to be humble. I will bless you at all times, Lord. Your praise shall forever be in my mouth. My soul will make its boast in you. I will magnify you, O Lord.

You are the high and lofty one who inhabits eternity. Your name is holy. You dwell in the high and holy place with those that are of a contrite and humble spirit. Thank you for your promise to revive the spirit of the humble and to revive the heart of the contrite ones. I want to be your humble and contrite servant at all times, Lord.

I humble myself before you, and as I draw near to you, Lord, I know you are drawing near to me. I cleanse my hands and purify my heart before you, and I humble myself in your sight, and I know you will lift me up. Thank you, Father, for delivering me from self-importance.

In Jesus' name I pray, Amen.

Scriptures: Romans 12:3; Proverbs 8:13; Proverbs 16:18-19; Proverbs 29:23; 1 John 2:15-16; Proverbs 28:25; Psalm 9:12; Psalm 34:1-3; Isaiah 57:15; James 4:7-10.

Personal Affirmation: I now realize that I have absolutely no reason to feel self-important. I am not better than anyone else. I humble myself, therefore, and will no longer let anything be done through strife and vainglory, but in lowliness of mind I will esteem others as being better than myself. (See Philippians 2:3.) I humble myself under God's almighty hand, and I know He will exalt me in due time.

Reflection: *"If you plan to build a tall house of virtues, you must first lay deep foundations of humility"* (St. Augustine).

37

Sorrow

My sorrow is continually before me.

(PSALM 38:17)

Central Focus: Sorrow is a form of psychological suffering that is caused by loss, disappointment, or some other negative circumstance. It involves sadness, grief, and sometimes regret. The God of all comfort does not want you to be sorrowful. He wants you to walk in newness of life, victory, and joy. Receive God's comfort into your life, and He will remove your sorrow and sadness.

Prayer: Lord God, you are my Shepherd. I shall not want. You make me lie down in green pastures and you lead me beside the still waters. You restore my soul and lead me in the paths of righteousness for your name's sake. Yea, though I walk through the valley of the shadow of death, I will fear no evil, for I know you are with me, and your rod and your staff comfort me. Thank you for the comfort you give to me, Father.

I know you will revive me and bring me up from the depths of sorrow. You will increase my greatness and comfort me on every side. Keep me walking in respectful fear of you and in the comfort of the Holy Spirit. Thank you for your Word, which gives me patience, comfort, and hope. Knowing your Word is my source for all good things. Thank you, Father.

You are the Father of my Lord Jesus Christ, the Father of mercies, and the God of all comfort, and I bless you. Thank you for the comfort you give to me during every tribulation, especially now, so that I would be able to comfort those who are in any kind of trouble by the comfort I receive from you. Thank you for filling me with comfort, Father. I am exceedingly joyful.

Hear, O Lord, and have mercy upon me. Be my helper. I believe you are turning my mourning and my sorrow into dancing. Thank you for removing the sackcloth from me and replacing it with gladness, to the end that my soul may sing praise to you and not be silent. O Lord my God, I will give thanks to you forever.

Thank you for replacing my mourning and my sorrow with joy. Thank you for the wonderful comfort you've provided for me. You are helping me to rejoice even in a time of sorrow. Surely goodness and mercy will follow me all the days of my life, and I will dwell in your house forever.

Thank you for the peace that Jesus has given to me. I will not let my heart be troubled or sorrowful any more.

In His mighty name I pray, Amen.

Scriptures: Psalm 23; Psalm 71:20-21; Acts 9:31; Romans 15:4; 2 Corinthians 1:3-4; 2 Corinthians 7:4; Psalm 30:10-12; Jeremiah 31:13; Psalm 23:6; John 14:27.

Personal Affirmation: Though I sorrow, it is not without hope. God's Word fills me with hope, and the God of all comfort has brought comfort and peace to me. He is with me each step of the way. He is turning my sorrow into joy, and I will always praise Him.

Reflection: *"Our greatest comfort in sorrow is to know that God is in control"* (Author unknown).

38

Spiritual-mindedness

For those who live according to the flesh set their minds on the things of the flesh, but those who live according to the Spirit, the things of the Spirit. For to be carnally minded is death, but to be spiritually minded is life and peace.

(ROMANS 8:5-6 NKJV)

Central Focus: Either we are carnally minded or we are spiritually minded. To be spiritually minded we must live close to the Lord. When we do so, He speaks to us and we are able to gain spiritual understanding and grow in faith. We must keep our minds fixed on the Lord, not on the things of this world. If we do so, we will experience His life and peace every day of our lives.

Prayer: Dear Father, thank you for enabling me to know you. Fill me with the knowledge of your will in all wisdom and spiritual understanding. It is my heartfelt desire to walk worthy of you, fully pleasing you and to be fruitful in every good work, as I increase in my knowledge of you. Thank you for strengthening me with all might according to your glorious power, with all patience and longsuffering with joyfulness.

I know that the natural man is unable to receive the things of your Spirit, because they are spiritually discerned. Help me to grow in spiritual discernment every day of my life. Thank you, Father, for blessing me with every spiritual blessing in heavenly places in Christ.

Thank you for filling me with the Holy Spirit. Help me to produce His spiritual fruit in all the relationships and responsibilities of my life. Help me to live and walk in the Spirit. It thrills me to know that the Spirit of life in Christ Jesus has set me free from the law of sin and death. I ask that you impart spiritual gifts to me, that I would be established in the faith.

Thank you for your Holy Spirit whose power enables me to be an effective witness for my Lord Jesus Christ. Help me always to be strong in you, Lord, and in the power of your might as I put on your whole armor, that I would always be able to stand against the works of the devil. I realize, Father, that I do not wrestle against flesh and blood, but against principalities, powers, the rulers of the darkness of this world, and spiritual wickedness in high places. Enable me to stand in the evil day, having girded my waist in truth and having on the breastplate of righteousness.

My feet are shod with the preparation of the gospel of peace, and I will take the shield of faith by which I will be able to quench all the fiery darts of the wicked. I will put on the helmet of salvation and the sword of the Spirit, which is your holy Word. I will always pray with all prayer and supplication in the Spirit and be watchful to this end with all perseverance and supplication for all saints.

Thank you for equipping me for spiritual warfare and spiritual-mindedness. I will let the mind of Christ always guide me.

In Jesus' name I pray, Amen.

Scriptures: Colossians 1:10-11; Colossians 1:11; 1 Corinthians 2:14; Ephesians 1:3; Galatians 6:22-23; Galatians 6:25; Romans 8:2; Romans 1:11; Acts 1:8; Ephesians 6:10-18; 1 Corinthians 2:16.

Personal Affirmation: I will walk in the Spirit so as not to fulfill the lusts of my flesh. I will live through the Spirit and mortify the deeds of my body. (See Romans 8:13.) I praise God for showing me that those who are led by the Spirit are truly His children. (See Romans 8:14.) Through the process of mental renewal (spiritual-mindedness), I will be able to prove what is God's good, acceptable, and perfect will. (See Romans 12:1-2.)

Reflection: *"Put your nose into the Bible every day. It is your spiritual food. And then share it. Make a vow not to be a lukewarm Christian"* (Kirk Cameron).

39

Stamina

But may the God of all grace, who called us to His eternal glory by Christ Jesus, after you have suffered a little while, perfect, establish, strengthen and settle you. To Him be the glory and the dominion for ever and ever. Amen.

(1 PETER 5:10-11 NKJV)

Central Focus: A person who possesses stamina is able to resist fatigue, illness, and hardship. Such a person is a good soldier of Jesus Christ. (See 2 Timothy 2:3.) Stamina is God's gift to you and it will keep you from weariness and confusion.

Prayer: Teach me your way, O Lord, and lead me on a clear path. Deliver me not over to my enemies. I will wait on you and be of good courage. In this way I know you will strengthen my heart and give me the stamina I need to face the challenges of life. I love you, O Lord, for I know that you preserve the faithful. Therefore, I will be of good courage, and I know you will strengthen me. Hallelujah!

Make me to understand the way of your precepts, Father. I will talk about all your wondrous works. Strengthen me according to your Word.

I will not fear nor be faint-hearted, for I know you are with me. I will not be dismayed, for I know you are my God. Thank you for your promise to strengthen me and uphold me. I ask that you would uphold me with the right hand of your righteousness. Thank you, Father. I know I can do all things through Christ who strengthens me.

Help me always to be steadfast and immoveable. I want to always abound in your work, O Lord, forasmuch as I know that my labor is not in vain in you. I will love you, O Lord, my strength. You are my rock and my deliverer. You are my God and my strength. I will always trust in you, for you are my buckler, the horn of my salvation, and my high tower.

Thank you for girding me with strength and stamina, O God, my strength and my redeemer. You are my light and my salvation. Whom shall I fear? You are the strength of my life. Of whom shall I be afraid? Thank you for your grace which is always sufficient for me. Your strength is made perfect in my time of weakness.

I praise you, Father, for giving me the strength and stamina I need to be a good soldier of Jesus Christ.

In His name I pray, Amen.

Scriptures: Psalm 27:11-14; Psalm 31:23-24; Psalm 119:27-28; Isaiah 41:10; Philippians 4:13;

1 Corinthians 15:58; Psalm 18:1-2; Psalm 18:32; Psalm 27:1; 2 Corinthians 12:9; 2 Timothy 2:3.

Personal Affirmation: God's strength is made perfect in my life when I am weak. He has completely restored stamina to me. I will take my stand upon His promises of strength. Spiritual stamina is enabling me to be physically strong and healthy. "But they that wait upon the Lord shall renew their strength; they shall mount up with wings as eagles; they shall run, and not be weary; and they shall walk, and not faith" (Isaiah 40:31).

Reflection: *"To learn strong faith is to endure great trials. I have learned my faith by standing firm amid severe testings"* (George Mueller).

40

Temperance

And everyone who competes for the prize is temperate in all things

(1 CORINTHIANS 9:25 NKJV)

Central Focus: To be temperate is to be self-controlled. A temperate person shows self-restraint in conduct and appetites. Temperance involves moderation in all things. God wants us to be temperate, and His Spirit enables us to practice temperance in all aspects of our lives. (See Galatians 5:22-23.)

Prayer: Teach me to be temperate at all times, Father. According to your divine power you have given unto me all things that pertain unto life and godliness as a result of knowing you. Thank you for calling me unto glory and virtue, and thank you so much for your great and precious promises that enable me to be a partaker of your nature, having escaped the corruption that is in the world through lust.

Therefore, giving all diligence, I will add virtue to my faith, knowledge to my virtue, temperance to my knowledge, patience to my temperance, godliness to my patience, brotherly kindness to my godliness, and love to my brotherly kindness.

Help me never to be self-willed. I do not want to ever be hasty, angry, given to wine, violent, or a lover of money. Instead, with your help I will be a lover of hospitality, a lover of good men, sober, just, holy, and temperate. I will hold fast the faithful word that you have taught me.

Thank you, Father, for not giving me a spirit of fear, but of power, love, and a sound mind. Because you have given me a sound mind, I am able to be moderate and temperate at all times. It is my desire to rejoice in you always, Lord, and to let my moderation be known unto all, for I know you are at hand, Lord.

I will not be anxious. Instead, in everything, by prayer and supplication with thanksgiving, I will let my requests be made known unto you. Thank you for your promise that your marvelous peace that surpasses all understanding will guard my heart and my mind through Christ Jesus.

Fill me afresh with the Holy Spirit, Father, so that I would produce His fruit of temperance in all the relationships and responsibilities of my life. Because I've been raised with Christ, I will seek those things that are above, where He sits at your right hand. I will set my affection on things above, not on things of this Earth, for I am dead and my life is hid with Christ in you.

Help me to put to death my members which are on the earth: fornication, uncleanness, passion, evil desire, and covetousness, which is idolatry.

I now put off anger, wrath, malice, blasphemy, and filthy language. I put on the new man who is renewed in knowledge. I put on tender mercies, kindness, humility, meekness and longsuffering.

In temperance, I will forbear with and forgive others. Above all things I will put on love, which is the bond of perfection, and I will let your peace rule in my heart while I let the Word of Christ dwell in me richly in all wisdom. Whatever I do in word or deed I will do all in the name of the Lord Jesus, giving thanks to you, Father.

I am grateful that you are showing me how to be temperate in all things.

In Jesus' name I pray, Amen.

Scriptures: 2 Peter 1:3-7; Titus 1:7-9; 2 Timothy 1:7; Philippians 4:4-5; Philippians 4:6-7; Galatians 5:22-23; Colossians 3:1-3; Colossians 3:5; Colossians 4:5-17.

Personal Affirmation: Through spiritual temperance and moderation, I will practice self-control in all my relationships and responsibilities. God is enabling me to be a temperate person. I will follow Him and walk in love and temperance as His dear child. "Let no corrupt communication proceed out of your mouth, but that which is good to the use of edifying, that it may minister grace unto the hearers. And grieve not the holy Spirit of God, whereby ye are sealed unto the day of redemption" (Ephesians 4:29-30).

Reflection: *"I am a spiritual being. . .. After this body is dead, my spirit will soar. I refuse to let what will rot to rule the eternal. I choose self-control. I will be drunk only by joy. I will be impassioned only by my faith. I will be influenced only by God. I will be taught only by Christ"* (Max Lucado).

41

Thriftiness

"You have sown much, and bring in little; you eat, but do not have enough; you drink, but you are not filled with drink; you clothe yourselves, but no one is warm; and he who earns wages, earns wages to put into a bag with holes."

(HAGGAI 1:6 NKJV)

Central Focus: Christian stewardship involves several things: thriftiness, carefulness, thoughtfulness, and a realization that everything we have belongs to God. Stewardship is the management of resources that are owned by another. A good manager does his best to be sure that money is spent wisely. A good manager makes certain that every investment is sound. We are responsible for the resources that God gives to us.

Prayer: Almighty God, thank you so much for what you have given to me. I realize that it all belongs to you. Help me always to take care of the resources and finances you have given to me. I always want to be a good steward in your service.

May I never forget to give when I have the opportunity to do so. As I give, I know you will give back to me. Good measure, pressed down, shaken together, and running over will be given to me. Thank you for this promise, Father. I do understand that with the same measure I use, it will be measured back unto me.

Help me to remember to bring the tithes into the storehouse, that there may be food in your house. Thank you for your promise to open the windows of Heaven as I do so, and pour out upon me a blessing that I will not be able to contain. Thank you also for assuring me that you will rebuke the devourer for my sake, so that he will not destroy anything in my life. Hallelujah!

Your Word declares: "He who sows sparingly will also reap sparingly, and he who sows bountifully will also reap bountifully. So let each one give as he purposes in his heart, not grudgingly or of necessity; for God loves a cheerful giver. And God is able to make all grace abound toward you, that you, always having all sufficiency in all things, may have an abundance for every good work."

Father, with your help I will be a bountiful sower. May I always be a cheerful giver. Thank you for your promise to make all grace abound toward me so that I will have an abundance for every good work. Thank you for Jesus who came to give me abundant life. I will walk in His abundance every day of my life, and I will be thrifty with regard to what He gives me.

I will seek first your kingdom and, as I do so, I know you will add all other things to my life. Thank you, Lord, for your faithfulness to me. I know you will take care of all my needs according to your riches in glory by Christ Jesus. I know I have no reason to ever worry about finances, because you are always taking good care of me.

I will never forget you, Father. I will always remember you as the Lord, my God. I know it is you who gives me the power to get wealth, so that you may establish your everlasting covenant. Thank you, Father.

Lord God, thank you for showing me that the love of money is the root of all evil. I realize that it can pierce me through with many sorrows. I will flee the love of money and follow after righteousness, godliness, faith, love, patience, and meekness. You are my Lord, and money is a blessing from your hands.

I trust in you, Lord, and I will do good with all you've given unto me. As a result, I know you will bless me. I will delight myself in you, and I know you will give me the desires of my heart. I have been young, and now am older, yet I have not seen the righteous forsaken, nor his seed begging bread. Thank you, Father, for always being merciful and giving toward me. Thank you for blessing your children and for blessing me. I will always endeavor to be your good steward. I want to be faithful to you and thrifty with all you give unto me.

In Jesus' name I pray, Amen.

Scripture: Luke 6:36; Malachi 3:10-12; 2 Corinthians

9:6-8; John 10:10; Matthew 6:33; Philippians 4:19; Matthew 6:31-32; Deuteronomy 8:18; 1 Timothy 6:10-11; Psalm 37:3-4; Psalm 37:25-26.

Personal Affirmation: Walking in freedom from any attachment to money or material things makes it possible for me to serve God more fully and to be a good steward of the financial blessings He bestows upon me. Realizing that everything I have is His to begin with, I will always be thrifty with my finances and responsible to Him in everything. I will be a cheerful giver and a good manager for my Lord and Master.

Reflection: *"A man's treatment of money is the most decisive test of his character—how he makes it and spends it"* (James Moffat).

42

Trusting God

Trust in the Lord with all your heart, and lean not on your own understanding; in all your ways acknowledge Him, and He shall direct your paths.

(PROVERBS 3:5-6 NKJV)

Central Focus: God will never violate your trust. He loves you so much that He will fulfill His promises to you. He is always trustworthy. Trust in God involves a firm belief or confidence in the honesty, integrity, reliability, and justice of our Creator. Trust involves faith, but it goes a step further than just believing. Trust in God is implicit certainty that He will do what He says in His Word. Trust Him and see what He is able to do for you.

Prayer: Heavenly Father, great is your faithfulness to me. Morning by morning new mercies I see. All I have needed your hand has provided. Great is your faithfulness unto me. I trust you implicitly; therefore, I cast all my cares upon you, for I know you care for me.

One of the promises of your Word assures me that all things in my life work together for good, and I know this is true from experience. I love you and I thank you for calling me according to your purpose. You have greatly blessed me, Father. I trust you and place all my hope in you. I know I will become like a tree that is planted by the rivers of water, a tree that spreads out its roots by the river, a tree that will not be affected by the heat, and a tree that always has green leaves—an evergreen tree. I will be a fruitful tree even in times of drought. Thank you for your promise that whatever I do will prosper.

Lord, you are my refuge and my fortress. You are my God, and I will always trust in you. I know you will surely deliver me from the snare of the fowler and from the perilous pestilence. Hallelujah! You will cover me with your feathers, and under your wings I will always safely abide and trust you at all times. Your truth shall be my shield and my buckler.

Abba-Father, I thank you that you always help me and deliver me. You have delivered me from the wicked, because I trust in you, and I always will. Therefore, I will not fear, though the Earth be removed and though the mountains be carried into the midst of the sea. When I am tempted to fear, I will replace the fear with trust in you. I have placed my complete trust in you, Father. Therefore, I will not fear what men can do to me. You have delivered my soul from death and my feet from falling. I will always walk before you in the light of the living.

Every one of your words, Lord, is pure. You are my

shield and the glory and lifter of my head. As I cry unto you with my voice, I know you hear me out of your holy hill. Thank you for removing all fear from my life. Lord, you are always on my side. Therefore, I will not fear. What can others do to me? I will trust in you rather than putting my confidence in people.

Thank you for the happiness I have as a result of trusting you. Looking unto Jesus, who is the author and finisher of my faith, I step out in trust and obedience. Through His grace I will trust and obey Him, for I know that there is no other way to be happy in Jesus. He said, "If you can believe, all things are possible to him who believes."

Through trusting in you I know that every day with Jesus is better than the day before. Thank you, Father.

In Jesus' name, Amen.

Scriptures: Lamentations 3:23; 1 Peter 5:7; Romans 8:28; Psalm 1:3; Psalm 91:2-4; Psalm 37:40; Psalm 46:2; Psalm 56:3-4; Proverbs 30:5; Psalm 118:6-8; Proverbs 16:20; Hebrews 12:2; Mark 9:23.

Personal Affirmation: I place my full trust and confidence in God, my Creator. I know He has good plans for me and that He will lead me to successful and abundant living. I can say unequivocally that He is always faithful to me and He has never let me down. My heart is filled with joy and happiness when I consider all He has done for me.

Reflection: *"Faith is a reasoning trust, a trust which reckons thoughtfully and confidently upon the trustworthiness of God"* (John R. Stott).

43

Unbelief

"Lord, I believe; help my unbelief!"

(MARK 9:24 NKJV)

Central Focus: Unbelief involves doubt, uncertainty, and double-mindedness. It is, of course, the opposite of belief and faith. Because we know that it is impossible to please God without faith (see Hebrews 11:6), we must make every effort to be sure that our faith remains firm at all times. Unbelief is a willful attitude; it is a positive refusal to believe. Take the leap of faith, and put all unbelief behind you as you stand upon the Word of God.

Prayer: O God, my Father, I do believe. Help me get rid of any and all unbelief. Jesus did not do as many mighty works as He might have because of the unbelief that existed in the people. As He rebuked the people for their unbelief, Jesus said, "If you have faith as a grain of mustard seed, you shall say unto this mountain, remove hence to yonder place; and it shall remove; and nothing shall be impossible to you."

This is mountain-moving faith, and I want such faith for myself, because I truly do believe what Jesus said: "Nothing shall be impossible to you." Hallelujah! Help me to be like Abraham who did not waver over your promises, but was strong in faith and always gave glory to you. Keep me from an evil heart of unbelief, Father, for I know that such a heart is one that departs from you. I never want to depart from you.

Any unbelief that I might harbor in my heart will prevent me from entering your rest, Father, and I know I need your rest. Thank you for providing it to me. Realizing that the just shall live by faith, I will walk in faith from this time forward. Through your grace I will obey your commandment to be strong and of good courage. I will not be afraid or dismayed, for I know you are always with me.

I will study, memorize, meditate upon, and pray your Word, because I know faith will come to me as I do so. Help me never to be double-minded, Father, because I know that a double-minded person is unstable in all his ways. Instead, I will pray in faith—the faith that comes from your Word.

I believe your Word which tells me that nothing is impossible with you. With your help I will build up myself through the most holy faith, and I will pray in the Holy Spirit. I will keep myself in your love, O Lord, and look for your mercy unto eternal life. Thank you so much for all the promises of your Word.

Laying aside all unbelief, therefore, I will walk by faith and not by sight. I choose to replace all unbelief with faith, knowing that all things are possible to him who believes. God, you are the strength of my heart and my portion forever. I believe in you, for you are the Lord, the God of all flesh, and nothing is too hard for you.

It thrills me to know that I have been born of you, Father. Equally thrilling is the knowledge that faith is the victory that overcomes the world.

My focus will be on growing in faith so as to please you more and more. This is my goal. As I pray your Word, I will pray the prayer the prayer of faith, and I know you will hear me and answer me. Thank you, Lord.

In the faithful name of Jesus I pray, Amen.

Scriptures: Mark 9:23; Matthew 13:58; Matthew 17:20; Romans 4:20; Hebrews 3:12; Hebrews 4:6; Romans 1:17; Joshua 1:9; Romans 10:17; James 1:5-8; Jude 20-21; 2 Corinthians 5:7; Mark 9:23; Psalm 73:26; Jeremiah 32:27; 1 John 5:4; James 5:15.

Personal Affirmation: I give my life afresh to the Lord. I choose to walk in faith, not in doubt and unbelief. My faith is based upon the promises of God's Word. I believe them, and I will trust God to fulfill them in my life. I will walk according to His Word and I will keep the faith. As a result, I know He will help me to grow in faith and in the grace of my Lord Jesus Christ.

Reflection: *"If one's conscience is willing to confess whatever sins have been committed, including the sin of unbelief, it will be sorrowful in a godly way, earnestly desiring the mercy of God"* (Watchman Nee).

44

Undisciplined Living

Whoever has no rule over his own spirit is like a city broken down, without walls.

(PROVERBS 25:28 NKJV)

Central Focus: Every disciple of Christ must live a disciplined lifestyle. The word discipline stems from disciple. When we follow Jesus, we develop self-control, character, orderliness, and efficiency. These attributes are characteristic of His disciples. Undisciplined living is never characteristic of a disciple of Christ.

Prayer: O God, my Father, I ask you to discipline and train me. Help me to remember all of your commandments and to do them. I never want to seek after my own heart and my own eyes. Instead, I will remember your commandments and I will be holy unto you.

Help me to keep control of my body and to bring it under subjection to you. Help me to keep my mind focused on the good things of life: whatsoever things that are honest, just, pure, lovely, and of good report. As your Word declares, "If there be any virtue, and if there be any praise, think on these things." I will do so, Father.

Teach me how to not be conformed to this world. Instead, I ask that you would help me to become completely transformed by the renewing of my mind, that I would be able to prove what is your good, perfect, and acceptable will. Thank you for all the help you give to me, Father.

Instead of having fellowship with the unfruitful works of darkness, I will reprove and expose them. Father, I desire to deny myself and to take up my cross daily as I follow you. Lord, I renounce the hidden things of dishonesty. I will not walk in craftiness nor handle your Word deceitfully. Denying ungodliness and worldly lusts, I will live soberly, righteously, and godly, as I look for that blessed hope and the glorious appearing of my great God and my Savior Jesus Christ.

Help me to be swift to hear, slow to speak, and slow to wrath, for I know that wrath never works your righteousness, Therefore , I will lay aside all filthiness and overflow of wickedness, and receive with meekness your implanted word, which is able to save my soul.

Thank you, Father.

Through your grace I will reckon myself to be dead unto sin, but alive to you through Jesus Christ, my Lord, and I will not let sin reign in my mortal body any longer. Teach me to do your will, for you are my God. Your Spirit is good. Lead me in the land of uprightness.

I choose to obey you and your Word, Father. Thank you for your promise to bless me as I learn to obey you. As I obey you, I experience your peace like a river and your righteousness as the waves of the sea. Thank you for your willingness to discipline and train me. I will be careful to do as you have commanded me. I will not turn aside either to the left or the right. As you lead me, I will walk in all the ways you have commanded me, that I may live and that it will be well with me. As a result, I know my days will be prolonged. Thank you, Father.

In Jesus' name I pray, Amen.

Scriptures: Numbers 15:39-40; 1 Corinthians 9:27; Philippians 4:8; Romans 12:2; Ephesians 5:11; Luke 9:23; 2 Corinthians 4:2; Romans 6:11-12; Psalm 143:10; Deuteronomy 11:26; Isaiah 48:18; Deuteronomy 5:32-33.

Personal Affirmation: From now on I will obey the Lord's voice, and I will walk in all the ways that He has commanded me, that it may be well with me. (See Jeremiah 7:23.) I submit myself to Him and I resist the devil. As I draw near to God, He draws near to me. I will cleanse my hands and purify my heart. I will humble myself in the sight of God, and I know He will lift me up. (See James 4:7-10.) I determine to be a disciplined follower of the Lord Jesus Christ from this point forward.

Reflection: *"Radical obedience to Christ is not easy. ... It's not comfort, not health, not wealth, and not prosperity in this world. Radical obedience to Christ risks losing all these things. But in the end, such risk finds its reward in Christ. And He is more than enough for us"* (David Platt).

45

Valor

Who through faith subdued kingdoms, worked righteousness, obtained promises, stopped the mouths of lions, quenched the violence of fire, escaped the edge of the sword, out of weakness were made strong, became valiant in battle, turned to flight the armies of the aliens.

(HEBREWS 11:33-34 NKJV)

Central Focus: To be valiant is to possess valor—a quality of marked courage and bravery. There were men in the Old Testament who were known as "mighty men of valor." According to God's Word, we can all be mighty people of valor who accomplish great feats for God through faith. It is faith that leads us to become valiant, as the above Scripture indicates, and it is faith that enables us to do the impossible.

Prayer: Lord God, in obedience to your Word I will wait on you and be of good courage. I know that as I do so, you will strengthen my heart and make me a person of valor. I will always hope in you. When I pass through the waters, you will be with me. When I go through the rivers, they will not drown me. When I walk through the fire, I will not be burned, because I know you are with me. Hallelujah!

My sense of valor comes from the certain knowledge that I can do all things through Christ who strengthens me. God, you are my refuge and underneath me are your everlasting arms. Thank you for your promise to thrust out the enemy before me. Dear Father, I ask that you would grant to me, according to the riches of your glory, strength in my inner being. Thank you for the truth that Christ dwells in my heart through faith. He is rooting and grounding me in love, and these promises assure me that I will be able to walk in valor. Thank you, Father.

Help me to always walk worthy of you, Lord. I want to fully please you, to be fruitful in every good work, and to increase in my knowledge of you. Strengthen me with all might according to your glorious power. I will always give thanks to you, Father, for qualifying me to be a partaker of the saints in the light and a mighty person of valor. Strengthen me according to your Word.

It is so wonderful to know that as I wait on you, my strength will be renewed and I shall mount up with wings like eagles. I will run and not be weary, and I will walk and not faint. Father, through your grace I will let my hands be strengthened, and I will be valiant. Thank you for your joy, Lord, for it truly is my strength. Help me to be strong in you always and in the power of your might.

You, Lord, are my rock, my fortress, and my deliverer. You are my strength, and I will always trust in you. You are my shield and the horn of my salvation. I praise you that you are my stronghold. Therefore, I will take up your armor. I know this will enable me to stand in the evil day and to be valiant in the face of all enemies.

Lord God, you are my light and my salvation. Whom shall I fear? You are the strength of my life. Of whom shall I be afraid? Your grace is sufficient for me. Your strength is made perfect in my weakness. Most gladly, therefore, I will rejoice because I know the power of Christ is resting upon me. He it is who makes me a mighty person of valor. I am complete in Him.

In Jesus' name I pray, Amen.

Scriptures: Psalm 27:14; Psalm 31:24; Isaiah 43:2; Philippians 4:13; Deuteronomy 33:27; Ephesians 3:16-17; Colossians 1:10-12; Psalm 119:28; Isaiah 40:31; 2 Samuel 2:7; Nehemiah 8:10; Ephesians 6:10; Psalm 18:2; Ephesians 6:13; Psalm 27:1; 2 Corinthians 12:9; Colossians 2:10.

Personal Affirmation: God enables me to be valiant in the face of all circumstances, including opposition. I want to be His mighty person of valor. I choose to be valiant as I walk with Him, realizing that His strength is made perfect in me. I can do all things through Him, because He strengthens me. I will not be afraid, because His love has cast out all fear from me. (See 1 John 4:18.)

Reflection: *"Valor is stability, not of legs and arms, but of courage and the soul"* (Michel de Montaigne).

46

Vocation

Be even more diligent to make your call and election sure, for if you do these things you will never stumble.

(2 PETER 1:10 NKJV)

Central Focus: A vocation is a calling, and God has called you into His service as a minister of the Gospel of Jesus Christ, an ambassador of His kingdom, and a fruit-bearing Christian. It is so wonderful to know that He has called us, and we must make every effort to be certain that we fulfill His calling in our lives. He has brought us into the priesthood of all believers.

Prayer: Father, thank you for calling me into your service. It is so wonderful to know that I am a partaker of your heavenly calling. Thank you for saving me and calling me with a holy calling, not according to my own works, but according to your own purpose and grace, which were given to me in Christ before the world began.

I pray that you would count me worthy of your calling

in my life. May I fulfill all the good pleasure of your goodness and the work of faith with power so that the name of my Lord Jesus Christ will be glorified, according to your grace. Forgetting those things that are behind and reaching forth unto those things that are before me, I press toward the mark for the prize of your high calling in Christ Jesus.

Father of glory, give me the spirit of wisdom and revelation in the knowledge of Christ. May the eyes of my understanding be enlightened, and may I know what the hope of my calling is and what are the riches of the glory of your inheritance in the saints. May I also experience the exceeding greatness of your mighty power.

Thank you for choosing me and calling me. I note that you do not call the wise and noble, but you have chosen the foolish things of the world to confound the wise, and you have chosen the weak to confound the mighty.

Father, help me to remain in the calling you have given to me. As your servant, I am actually a free person. It is my privilege to be a servant of Christ. I was bought with the price of His shed blood. Therefore, I will always be His servant, not the servant of men. I will abide in Him. Thank you for your Word, which assures me that your gifts and calling in my life are irrevocable.

Jesus said that many are called, but few are chosen. Thank you for both calling and choosing me, Lord. I did not choose you, but you chose me and ordained me, that I should go forth and bear fruit. Thank you for your promise that the fruit I bear will remain and that whatever I ask in Jesus' name, you will give. Praise the Lord!

In Jesus' name I pray, Amen.

Scripture: Hebrews 3:1; 2 Timothy 1:9; 2 Thessalonians 1:11-12; Philippians 3:14; Ephesians 1:17-19; 1 Corinthians 1:26-27; 1 Corinthians 7:20-23; Romans 11:29; Matthew 20:16; John 15:15-16.

Personal Affirmation: I am so thankful that God has chosen me, and I will always be happy in His service. As a soul-winner, I will reach out to the lost. I will produce the fruit of the Holy Spirit in all the relationships and responsibilities of my life. (See Galatians 5:22-23.) My goal is to be a fruit-bearing Christian for the rest of my life.

Reflection: *"All vocations are intended by God to manifest His love in the world"* (Thomas Merton).

47

Wholeness

They that are whole have no need of the physician, but they that are sick: I came not to call the righteous, but sinners to repentance.

(MARK 2:17)

Central Focus: Wholeness involves perfection and holiness, without which no one will see the Lord. Such qualities come from God who is perfect in His holiness. Jesus, who knew no sin, became sin for us, that we might become the righteousness of God through Him. (See 2 Corinthians 5:21.) He is our righteousness, our wholeness, and our perfection.

Prayer: Thank you for giving me wholeness through Christ, dear Father. I am complete in Him. All of your fullness dwells in Jesus, and He dwells within me! He is before all things and by Him all things consist. He is the head of the Body, His Church. You are my lamp, O Lord, and you are enlightening my darkness. You enable me to run through a troop and to leap over a wall. Your way is perfect, and your Word is tried. You are a mighty shield to me. You are my rock, my strength, and my power, and you make my way perfect. Thank you for the wholeness you are imparting unto me.

Thank you for making my feet like hinds' feet and setting me upon high places. Thank you for teaching my hands to war. You have given me the shield of your salvation, and your gentleness has made me great. You have enlarged my steps under me so that my feet will never slip. Thank you for all these blessings, dear Lord.

Your Word is perfect, Father. It converts the soul, and it is sure, making wise the simple. Your Word rejoices my heart. It is so pure that it enlightens my eyes. I love you and I love your Word. Your Word is leading me into perfection and wholeness. Thank you, Lord. Through your grace I will be whole and perfect like you are.

Help me never to forget how important love is. There is no fear in love, for God's perfect love casts out all fear. I believe your Word, which says, "He that fears is not made perfect in love." Make me perfect in love, Father, for I know it is the most excellent way of all.

Help me to be sober and vigilant, Father, because I know that the enemy, as a roaring lion, walks about and seeks whom he may devour. Through your power I will resist him steadfast in the faith. God of all grace, thank you for calling me unto eternal glory by Christ Jesus. I know that after I've suffered awhile you will make me perfect, and you will establish, strengthen, and settle me. Thank you, Father, for enabling me to walk in wholeness every step of my way.

In Jesus' name I pray, Amen.

Scriptures: Colossians 2:10; Colossians 2:9; Colossians 1:17-18; 2 Samuel 22:29-33; 2 Samuel 22:34-37; Psalm 19:7-8; Matthew 5:48; 1 John 4:18; 1 Corinthians 12:31; 1 Peter 5:8-10.

Personal Affirmation: God is making me completely whole. (See John 7:23.) He is perfecting me. In my own flesh there is no righteousness or wholeness, but through Christ I am made whole. He is changing me into His image. I need Him. Without Him I can do nothing, but through Him I can do all things.

Reflection: *"We were created to be expressions of the goodness and wholeness of God"* (Erwin McManus).

48

Will of God

And the world is passing away, and the lust of it; but he who does the will of God abides forever.

(1 JOHN 2:17 NKJV)

Central Focus: The Bible contains the whole counsel of God, and it reveals His will to us. He speaks to us through His Word. To follow His will, therefore, we must walk in the truth of His Word. We are able to ascertain God's general will for us, and we are able even to ascertain His specific will for us in given situations. Whatever the case, we must endeavor to follow His will at all times.

Prayer: Heavenly Father, I thank you for revealing your will to me through your Word. Help me to obey you and follow your will at all times. In everything I will give thanks, because I know this is your will in Christ Jesus concerning me.

I realize, Father, that my thoughts and your thoughts

are not the same. This is also true regarding my ways and your ways. As the heavens are higher than the Earth, so are your ways higher than my ways and your thoughts are higher than my thoughts. Your Word helps me to bridge this gap. Thank you, Lord.

I will pursue the knowledge of you, Father. I thank you that your going forth is established as the morning. I know you will come to me like the rain, like the latter and former rain to the Earth. I thank you for your Word, which reveals your will to me. It is a lamp to my feet and a light to my path. Your testimonies are my delight and my counselors.

Your Word shall not depart from my mouth. I will meditate in it both night and day, and I will observe to do according to all that is written therein. In so doing, I know you will make my way prosperous and give me good success. Thank you, Father.

All Scripture is given by your inspiration, Father, and it is profitable for doctrine, for reproof, for correction, for instruction in righteousness, that I may be complete, thoroughly equipped for every good work. Thank you, Lord, for revealing the mystery of your will to me. I choose to redeem the time, because I know the days are evil. Through your grace I will not be unwise, but I will understand your will. Help me to walk circumspectly at all times.

As a servant of Christ, I will do your will from my heart. With good will I will serve you, knowing that you will bless me as I do good to others. Thank you, Lord.

In the name of Jesus I pray, Amen.

Scriptures: 1 Thessalonians 5:18; Isaiah 55:8-9; Hosea 6:3; Psalm 119:105; Psalm 119:24; Joshua 1:8; 2 timothy 3:16-17; Ephesians 1:9; Ephesians 5:15-17; Ephesians 6:6-7.

Personal Affirmation: As I ascertain God's will for my life, I will walk in His ways and His will at all times. I will put aside my own will in favor of His. His will is perfect; my will is imperfect. I will study His Word to show myself approved unto Him, and I will rightly divide His Word. (See 2 Timothy 2:15.) His Word is truth. His Word is a light unto my path. His Word will never fail. I cherish His Word at all times.

Reflection: *"Outside the will of God there is nothing I want and in the will of God there is nothing I fear"* (A.W. Tozer).

Yielding to the Lord

Submit yourselves therefore to God. Resist the devil, and he will flee from you.

(JAMES 4:7)

Central Focus: Yielding to the Lord involves death to self. It is a surrender of our wills to His. The power of the Holy Spirit enables us to yield to Him. We do so because we know He is always faithful to us. Yielding to Him entails obedience to Him, submission to Him, and surrendering everything we have to Him, because we know it is His already.

Prayer: Heavenly Father, through your grace I will let the word of Christ dwell in me richly in all wisdom. I will teach and admonish others in psalms and hymns and spiritual songs, singing unto you with grace in my heart. I will yield my entire life, heart, and soul to you, and whatever I do in word or deed, I will do all in the name of the Lord Jesus, giving thanks to you, Father, by Him.

As the friend of Jesus, I will do whatever He commands me to do. I choose to walk in obedience to you. I delight myself in your Word, Father, and I will never forget its teachings. Make me to understand the way of your precepts, so shall I talk of all your wondrous works.

Through your grace I will deny myself and take up my cross daily and follow you. I will yield my life completely to you, for I know that whosoever will save his life shall lose it, but whosoever will lose his life for your sake, the same shall save it. You have shown me that there is no advantage in gaining the whole world and losing myself. Thank you, Lord.

It is in you that I live, move, and have my being. I am your offspring, and you are my Father. Hallelujah! I trust in you, Lord, and I will always endeavor to do good. I will delight myself in you, and I know you will give me the desires of my heart. I commit my way unto you and trust implicitly in you. Thank you for your promise that you will bring forth my righteousness as the light.

Father, your Word tells me to obey your voice. As I do so, I know you will be my God. I choose to walk in all the ways you have commanded me to do, that it may be well with me. To know that I know you I must keep your commandments, for I realize that whoever keeps your Word experiences your perfect love within. I choose to abide in Christ and to walk as He walked.

Teach me to do your will, Father, for you are my

God. Your Spirit is good. Lead me in the land of uprightness. Father, I will be careful to do as you have commanded me. I will not turn aside to the right or to the left. I will walk in all the ways you have commanded me to do, that I may live and that it will be well with me. Thank you for your promise of longevity, Lord.

Have mercy upon me, O God, according to your lovingkindness: according to the multitude of your tender mercies blot out my transgressions. Wash me thoroughly from my iniquity and cleanse me from my sins. I acknowledge my transgressions, and my sin is ever before me. Create in me a clean heart, O God, and renew a right spirit within me. Cast me not away from your presence and do not take your Holy Spirit from me. Restore unto me the joy of your salvation, and uphold me with Your free spirit.

I will always seek first your kingdom and your righteousness, knowing that as I do so, you will add all other things to me.

I pray in Jesus' name, Amen.

Scriptures: Colossians 3:16-17; John 15:14; Psalm 119: 16, 27; Luke 9:23-25; Acts 17:28; Psalm 37:3-6; Jeremiah 7:23; 1 John 2:3-6; Psalm 143:10; Deuteronomy 5:32-33; Psalm 51:1-3, 10-12; Matthew 6:33.

Personal Affirmation: "I am crucified with Christ: nevertheless I live; yet not I, but Christ liveth in me: and the life which I now live in the flesh I live by the faith of the Son of God, who loved me, and gave himself for me" (Galatians 2:20). I yield everything I am and have to the Lord. He will always come first in my life.

Reflection: *"Let God have your life; He can do more with it than you can"* (Dwight L. Moody).

Yoked Together with the Lord

"Come to Me, all you who labor and are heavy laden, and I will give you rest. Take My yoke upon you and learn from Me, for I am gentle and lowly in heart, and you will find rest for your souls. For My yoke is easy and My burden is light."

(MATTHEW 11:28-30 NKJV)

Central Focus: Jesus is everything to us, and He invites us to come to Him and take up His yoke, which He explains is easy and light. To be a yoke-fellow with Him we must stop trying to do everything in our own strength. We must learn to lean on Him and work with Him. This will result in rest for our souls. Remember that God shall supply all your need according to His riches in glory by Christ Jesus. (See Philippians 4:19.)

Prayer: Abba-Father, thank you for Jesus who is my Savior and Lord. He is the King of kings and the Lord of lords. I am His, and He is mine. I can do all things through Him because He strengthens me to do so. I am more than a conqueror through Him. I will cooperate with Him at all times.

As I abide in Jesus and He abides in me, I will bear much fruit, for without Him I can do nothing. He promises me that if I abide in Him and let His words abide in me, I will ask what I desire and my prayers will be answered. There is another prayer promise that I will always remember as well: where two or three are gathered together in the name of Jesus, He is always there.

You are light, Father, and there is no darkness whatsoever in you. It is my heart's desire to walk together with you in the light so that I will have fellowship with you and work together with you. Thank you for the blood of Jesus, which cleanses me from all sin.

Thank you for Jesus who is a friend that sticks closer than a brother. I will walk with Him and work with Him. I praise you for making all grace abound toward me, that I would have all sufficiency in all things and abundance for every good work. All of my sufficiency comes from you, Father. It is wonderful to know that I am more than a conqueror through Christ.

Jesus is working with me as He did with the early disciples, and He is confirming God's Word with signs following. It is wonderful to work with Jesus. He is my friend, my brother, my co-worker, and my helper. Help me not to receive your grace in vain. Hear me, O Lord, and have mercy upon me; Lord, be my helper. You have turned my mourning into dancing and girded me with gladness to the end that my soul may sing praise to you and not be silent. O Lord my God, I will give thanks unto you forever. Thank you for being my helper and my co-worker.

Yes, you, O Lord, are my helper, and I will never fear what others can do to me. I thank you that Jesus Christ is the same yesterday, today, and forever. Thank you, God, for allowing me to labor together with Him and you.

In His name I pray, Amen.

Scriptures: Revelation 19:16; 1 Corinthians 3:23; Philippians 4:13; Romans 8:37; John 15:4-5, 7; Matthew 18:20; 1 John 1:5-7; Proverbs 18:24; 2 Corinthians 9:8; 2 Corinthians 3:5; Romans 8:37; Mark 16:20; 2 Corinthians 6:1; Psalm 30:10-12; Psalm 54:4; Hebrews 13:6-8; 1 Corinthians 3:9;

Personal Affirmation: I take the Lord's yoke upon me, as I learn of Him. How thankful I am that His yoke is easy and His burden is light. He is my co-worker. I will work with Him. I will always remember these words: "The battle is the Lord's" (1 Samuel 17:47). Knowing this, I take my rest in Him. It is a joy to have fellowship with Him and to walk with Him hand in hand each step of the way.

Reflection: *"He takes us as we are, and makes us more than we ever imagined"* (Neill F. Marriott).

Afterword

Writing the eight books in this series has been a joy and privilege for me, for it has enabled me to grow in the grace and knowledge of the Lord while blessing others. If you have not read the other seven books, let me take this opportunity to encourage you to do so. All the books have been published by Bridge-Logos, Inc. I list each book below along with a brief quotation from each:

1. *Prayers That Change Things*. "For these reasons and so many others you must learn to pray God's Word. The expression, "Prayer changes things," takes on new meaning when you do so. Indeed, these prayers really do change things. Most importantly, they change you and the way you look at things in your life.

2. *Prayers That Change Things in Your Relationships*. "Prayer helps us build our relationships, and relationships are so important in our lives. In fact, they are the part of our lives that will live on forever, because love never dies. What we invest in our relationships now will pay dividends forever."